Enjoy the Girls
Elaine Colton
September, 2010

The Newport Girls

A Memoir

Elaine Colton

iUniverse, Inc.
New York   Bloomington

The Newport Girls
A Memoir

Copyright © 2010 Elaine Colton

All rights reserved. No part of this book may be used or reproduced by any means, graphic, electronic, or mechanical, including photocopying, recording, taping or by any information storage retrieval system without the written permission of the publisher except in the case of brief quotations embodied in critical articles and reviews.

iUniverse books may be ordered through booksellers or by contacting:

iUniverse
1663 Liberty Drive
Bloomington, IN 47403
www.iuniverse.com
1-800-Authors (1-800-288-4677)

Because of the dynamic nature of the Internet, any Web addresses or links contained in this book may have changed since publication and may no longer be valid. The views expressed in this work are solely those of the author and do not necessarily reflect the views of the publisher, and the publisher hereby disclaims any responsibility for them.

ISBN: 978-1-4502-3106-0 (pbk)
ISBN: 978-1-4502-3108-4 (cloth)
ISBN: 978-1-4502-3107-7 (ebook)

Library of Congress Control Number: 2010907559

Printed in the United States of America

iUniverse rev. date: 6/1/10

I dedicate this book to Arlene "Leenie" Callahan Dovel, who pretty much was the wind beneath my wings all through my journey, and still is.

Contents

Introduction ix
The Beginning 1
Middletown 3
Rogers High 1956 to 1959 6
Rocky 23
Marriage #1 25
Marriage #2 27
Marriage #3 29
Healing 32
Turning Fifty 33
Friends Do the Darndest Things 38
Year 2000 42
The Love of My Life 43
2009 44
Mary and Me 47
Gretchen and Me 49
Marianne 51
Ginny 52
Turning Fifty 53

My Mom and Me 56

Back To 2009 61

Gretch, Me, and the Movies 63

Leenie and Me 64

Arlene Callahan Dovel—My Story 70

Gretchen Buxbaum Kelly—My Story 74

Mary O'Hanley Clark—My Story 79

Nancy Ellis Carroll—My Story 85

Virginia McGinn Regan—My Story 88

Barbara Nelson Watterson—My Story 91

Lynn Harvey Summers—My Story 93

Eileen O'Reilly Daschbach—My Story 95

Linda Simmons—My Story 97

Kathy Ewart Keay—My Story 99

Ellen Parsonage Wright—Crossing over the Newport Bridge 105

The End 107

Epilogue 108

Introduction

I was born on November 14, 1941 to Roslyn and Lester Glickman in Malden, Massachusetts. I have no recollection of how we got to Alexandria, Virginia, but people say my father had a very secret job, as a civilian for the Navy. To this day, I have no idea what he did for sure, but rumor had it he had something to do with the Underwater Ordinance Laboratory, and he always had a torpedo (miniature) on his desk. My father graduated from MIT at age twenty, and I guess he was considered a very smart man. I remember seeing very big black-and-white pictures of the Iwo Jima Memorial when I was six or seven years old. It was on a flatbed truck going down Pennsylvania Avenue in Washington, DC. It wasn't until many years later that I realized this was the statue that now stands beside Arlington National Cemetery, and it must have been right after World War II. My father was a photography buff and loved to take interesting pictures like that.

There were also pictures of big white and grey mushrooms in the sky; and I learned, when I grew up, that my father had traveled to Eniwetok and Bikini for the first atom bomb tests. It stands to reason that exposure to radiation might have contributed to my father's death, many years later. The most unusual part of this is that I have no memory of my father having been gone—I must have been very young.

There is not one family member alive who has any recollection of how my father met my mom. They met somewhere in Massachusetts, where they both were from. I remember my father telling me that he later proposed to my mother in a rowboat on the reservoir in Newton, Massachusetts. I am the last person to judge what makes a person choose to marry someone, but both families disliked each other intently. It must have been very challenging for my parents in the beginning.

My earliest memories of my mom are that she was pretty, funny, strong, and very dramatic. My uncle told me that my mother wanted to become an actress and go to New York, but that never happened. She did join the Little Theatre in Alexandria, Virginia, and I remember, just a short time before they took her away, that she was in a play and was a wonderful actress.

How she got sick, I'll never know, but she did. I don't know why they chose to do it this way, but one day there was a knock on our apartment door. And when I opened it, there was my mother's oldest brother and two policemen, and they took my mother away. I can't remember where my father was or who stayed with my young brother and me, but that was the first defining moment in my life.

With Grandpa Glickman

The rest of this tale really begins at the end, in 2009. Transformation occurs in many ways; you never know when a transformational experience will hit you.

My transformational experience happened going over the Newport Bridge in June of 2009. I looked down at Narragansett Bay—the flurry of sailboats scattered in the blue water and the Navy War College—and I began to cry. I was overcome by something, and I wasn't sure what it was or why it was happening and at that moment. I didn't understand what was about to happen over the next four days. I didn't know it then, but I know it now; the fact that most of the girls of my youth were going to be here was extraordinary, and I needed to tell the story of the Newport girls.

So ... now to the beginning.

I suppose having a dysfunctional childhood is not unusual, but when I had mine, almost sixty years ago, the word "dysfunctional" was only used to describe some piece of equipment that didn't work. My family was just a mess. As far as I could tell, my job was to survive it, flourish, and against all odds, turn out okay.

This is the story of my survival. It's about love and loss, mistakes, failures, and triumphs and the wonderful women, **The Newport Girls,** who were in my life, one way or another, as I made this journey.

The Beginning

It all began almost sixty-nine years ago. I guess my birth was pretty much no big deal. I had a mom and a dad, and for four years, until my brother came along, I was pretty much the center of their world. The truth is I'm making it all up, and until the doorbell rang and the police took my mother away, everything is made up—I have no memory. My journey began at nine, when my mother was gone from my life. I truly believed she was gone forever.

What does a nine-year-old know about snake pits, double lobotomies, and mental illness? All my brother and I knew was that we didn't have a mother anymore. Many years later, as I tried to understand why my mother was the way she was, I had a wonderful uncle (her youngest brother) who did his best to explain that back in the very late 1940s, professionals had very few methods of managing mental illness. Lobotomies were the final step if all else failed. I cringe to think what my mother must have endured. Today, she would be on medication and most likely would be able to live a very useful, creative life, but this is now and that was then. So off my mother went, never to return the way I'd dreamed my mother would be.

I was the lucky one. I was sent to the "nice aunt." My mother's oldest sister lived in Massachusetts and was wonderful to take me in. My uncle owned a men's clothing store and my aunt was a stay-at-home mom. They had two great sons I loved and looked up to. For two years out of my childhood, I lived in the "Cleaver Family."

I was so loved and cared for and when I left, I think my heart was broken for the second time; I'd lost my second mother and I was only eleven. My brother was not so lucky. At age five, he went to live with the "mean uncle," and he paid the price for it. That uncle was married to my father's oldest sister, and as far as I can see, there was very little love and nurturing for my baby brother.

Why do I still cry because I could not take care of him when he was little? That lack of love and family nurturing has definitely contributed to his life's being less than fulfilled.

Who knows? If we'd stayed together those few years, life might have turned out differently, but that's another story.

Fast forward to 1952. My mother was away in some mental hospital, and my father, who worked as an engineer for the Navy, was transferred to Newport, Rhode Island. By no fault of my own, the good aunt decided it was time for me to live with my dad. As a child, I blamed him for my mother's illness and the total chaos our family was in. I didn't call him "Daddy" until almost four decades later. I think I was so deeply sad that I had to leave my aunt and all the goodness she gave me that I blamed my father for everything. I suppose the mean uncle decided the same thing, and my brother and I left the most stable homes we had ever known (I can't speak for him, but I was devastated to leave my aunt) and went to live with our father in Middletown, Rhode Island. I was eleven and my brother was seven. We never bonded, my brother and me, because from that point on, as a child, the name of the game for me was survival. It's taken me over fifty years to forgive myself for not being able to be the mother my brother never had. My heart still hurts from time to time because my life has been so blessed and his took a different direction.

Middletown

If you'd never been to the Island, you'd only think there was Newport, but those of us who lived there knew there were three towns. We lived in Middletown, aptly named since it was between Newport and Portsmouth. In those days, there wasn't even a bridge to Jamestown. You had to ferry across Narragansett Bay. Fall River, Massachusetts, and Providence had bridges from the Island, and if we ever crossed them it was a big deal. For the most part, we lived in our own little world on the Island. If we ever met anyone from out of town, we always said we lived in Newport—it was easier.

Leenie: 1952

It all began at our little house on Jude Street. It was small, but safe. I was strong and bold and I decided to be the mom. To the best of my ability, I took care of myself, our home, my brother, and my father and went to school. It seems quite daunting when I think about it, but back then I never thought about it. I just did it.

To my utter delight, there were two nice families who lived across the street and they both had daughters: Jean was younger than I and Betty was older, but just like the fabled Goldilocks, I thought Arlene was just right. She was my age and nice; how lucky that our fathers worked together. Leenie was my first "BFF." The Callahan's (Leenie's family) seemed so normal compared to mine; there were two parents, a sister, and a dog named Buttons. I thought she had the perfect life. No one knows what goes on inside, but from the outside looking in her life was idyllic. She wanted me as her friend too; even though I thought my home life was a mess.

The truth is, she really was the first Angel in my life, and our almost fifty-eight-year friendship has been the most important I have ever had. She saved me from the drudgery of my home life and helped me create an awesome world outside that gave me hope that there might be a possibility of survival.

I know this was way before I knew what a best friend was, but I picked one, and it was Arlene. From my point of view, she had everything—a normal family and a dog—and she was cute. She has far more memories than I do, and you will hear her story as this unfolds, but here's who she was for me.

Arlene was my sixth-, seventh-, and eighth-grade buddy. We got bused to school, and each day was an escape from my life the minute we started walking toward the bus. I was not a great student, but I got lost in school. I had a crush on Mr. Pelletier, our English teacher, and loved making relief maps out of flour and water and paint in my geography class with our great red-headed teacher, Mr. Kelly. I don't even know if Arlene and I were in any classes together; I just knew that her presence was always with me. Even though we were young, I knew she liked me for who I was, and over the years, no matter what breaks in relationships, losses, husbands, divorces, kids, grandkids, and having and not having, she was the dearest friend a girl could ever ask for in a lifetime.

Leenie & Me At Easter

My greatest claim to fame during that time was being chosen to be the Valedictorian of our eighth-grade class. I haven't a clue why, but it was an honor I will always cherish. I knew I had a white dress with a crinoline under it, but I have no memory as to whether my mother was home with us or not or who bought me the dress. I do remember walking up onto the stage and speaking my first word: "Welcome." The sweeter memories of those years were playing in the cornfields behind Leenie's house and just being joyful together.

Rogers High
1956 to 1959

Fast forward to Rogers High and the really big years, because that's where the Newport Girls expanded. It was no longer just Leenie and me, but we chose some of the most amazing girls to be our friends. At that time, clearly, we had no idea how anyone would turn out, but to the one, each has an incredible story of how her life evolved. Through all the challenges and tragedies, they have turned out to be powerful women in their own right. My story is the big picture; later you will hear from some of them in their own words.

My mother came home from time to time from whatever hospital she was in, and it was very hard to have her around, considering her underlying illness. My goal was to make "the great escape" whenever I could. Unfortunately, my brother incurred her mental and physical abuse because unlike me, he didn't have the will, strength, or age to find his way. It has taken me over half a century to forgive myself for not saving him. All my energy was expended in saving myself.

Not until over fifty years later did I realize and honor the fact that I truly was my mother's daughter. I could not have survived without her grit, talent, and determination. She survived as long as she did by being determined to live as good a life as she could under all the conditions. She truly was a victim of her generation—I was not. Had she not been ill, she could have been extraordinary, but given the medicine and practices of her time, she was a true marvel. I say this even though living through it and with her was a nightmare at the time.

So back to high school. I don't know how or why these were the girls that would be a part of my life forever. Why did I choose them? Why did they choose me? I could probably make up something that would sound profound, but why bother? We just did!

Here they are, in no particular order, because after Arlene, everyone else was frosting on the cake: Gretchen, Judy, Lynn, Marianne, Mary, Nancy, Ginny, Eileen, Kathy, Linda, and for some period of time, Mary Mac, Sally, Rosemary, Barbara, and maybe a few others. These were the Newport Girls.

Freshman year probably had the biggest impact on all of us. Gretch was chosen to write "Teen Scene" in our daily paper, *The Newport Daily News*. I'll bet our names appeared in many a column. Leenie, Gretchen, Mary, Judy, and I modeled at our local department store, The Boston Store on Thames Street. We were called Junior Debs, and our pictures were displayed throughout the store. I can't explain how that came about, either, but we did it for years, and I think we thought we were local stars. Another big event that happened in our high school was called the Breck Coiffeur Cavalcade. The Breck shampoo company chose our school to participate in the event. We were interviewed and chosen because of our hair. I was not one of the Breck Girls, but Leenie was one of the lucky ones and represented the Gibson Girl. She wore a beautiful white velvet gown with a big picture hat, and she carried a parasol. Mary also represented our group. The girls chosen appeared throughout *Life* magazine and were on the cover, shampooing their hair. Those of us not part of this were probably a little jealous, but in the end, our gang was represented, and we truly thought this was a big deal—it was.

The one decision that shaped who Leenie, Judy, and I were in high school was our decision to try out for Pep Nite. Pep Nite belonged to the seniors, and it was totally unheard of for any freshman to even think of auditioning, but as Leenie writes later on, we must have had show biz, or just daring, in our blood. We went to try out and we made it!

So on some spring night in 1956, three fourteen-year-old girls, dressed in our fathers' zoot suits and white bucks, with mops on our heads and black thick eyebrows, took the stage for Rogers High School Pep Nite. We brought down the house with our pantomime and lip-synching to "You Are So Rare to Me" and "Going Crazy (bahbadobabado)," made famous on *Your Show of Shows* by The Haircuts; Sid Caesar, Carl Reiner, and Howard Morris. Like Sally Fields said many years later, "You love me—you really love me." They didn't just love us—we blew them away, and our picture appeared on the front page of *The Newport Daily News* the next day with a caption that said "Show Stoppers: Heaviest applause during Pep Nite performance at RHS went to these three freshman girls." It was very cool for three girls who had just barely made it into puberty. Thus, for the following three years of high school, we were known as The Three Haircuts; we felt pretty special about that.

I'd lied about my age when I was fifteen so I could get a job at the Drive-In Theatre that was across the street from where we lived. I watched the wonderful world of fantasy five nights a week after I collected tickets at the front gate. I loved it—it gave me a break from the reality of my life. At sixteen, I was very persistent and got the "cream of the crop" job after high school: I became a first-class scooper at the Newport Creamery.

Leenie got her license at sixteen. My father never let me get mine because he said Leenie drove, and given the logic of the day, that meant I didn't need to. Mary became a head cheerleader at school, and Nancy was on her team. Mary could bend in half backward, and I was always in awe of her athletic ability. Lynn's family had a wonderful lodge we could go to once in a while for a girl's weekend, and as we grew older, boys were allowed to come for a day and then go home. We were, after all, "the good girls"; no hanky-panky for this group. I remember being asked to go steady by my first flame, a darling boy who was two years younger than I, on one of those glorious weekends at Miskiania (that was the name of the lodge). I think we broke up on the following Monday—I never went steady again.

The Newport Girls

The Newport Girls at My House

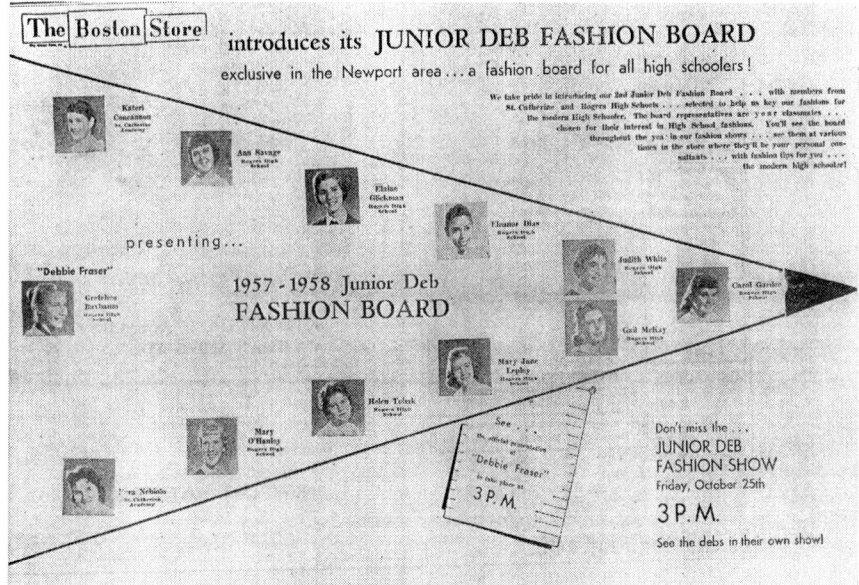

The Boston Store Junior Debs
Reprinted courtesy of The Newport Daily News

Elaine Colton

Pep Nite - The Three Haircuts 1956
Reprinted courtesy of The Newport Daily News

Teen Scene
Reprinted courtesy of The Newport Daily News

The Newport Girls

Some of the Third Beach Gang
Reprinted courtesy of The Newport Daily News

Elaine Colton

More Bathing Beauties—1950s Style
Reprinted courtesy of The Newport Daily News

The Newport Girls

BATHING BEAUTIES — These teenagers at Hazard's Beach are, from left, Nancy Ellis of 23 Honeyman Ave., Middletown, Lila O'Hanley of 17 Malbone Road, Eileen Hussey of 18 Annandale Terrace, and Mary O'Hanley of 18 Boulevard, Middletown. (Daily News Photo)

The Hazards Beach Girls
Reprinted courtesy of The Newport Daily News

Elaine Colton

Gretchen

The Gang in a Serious Moment

Elaine Colton

The Halls of Rogers High

It Was Cool to Hang out with the Boys

Pajama Party

Leenie as a Breck Girl

Mary as a Breck Girl

Along the Cliff Walk

Skating on the Cement Mixer Pond
Reprinted courtesy of The Newport Daily News

We all graduated from high school, and of course I was expected to go off to college even though I really didn't want to. By some curse or miracle, off I went to Gator Land to be a University Of Florida coed! It really was a very quick decision on my father's part. My grandmother lived in St. Petersburg, and I guess he thought I'd be close to some family. What culture shock it was for me. There were girls with southern accents. Some of the girls from Georgia spoke with such a drawl I could hardly understand them. And there were cute boys all over the place and all kinds of distractions, including a mother who followed me to Florida and practically had a nervous breakdown before my eyes. I dropped out of school, returned home to Newport, and at eighteen, had no idea what to do with my life.

My only real work experience up to that point in my life was working at the drive-in and the Creamery. Neither of these past adventures seemed like a life path I wanted to travel, but while I was searching for the thing to do, the Creamery was happy to have me back.

Rocky

And then came Rocky. Let me tell you that Rocky was the *most* eligible bachelor in Newport at the time (well, in my eyes anyway). He had been a Marine, he was an established businessman, and he was charming, Catholic, and thirty! I was charming, Jewish, and eighteen. My father had a fit because the age difference was a very big deal to him, and Jewish girls did not date older Catholic men, but Rocky and I soon became a "couple" on the Newport scene. Leenie was off at secretarial school, Mary was in nursing school, and I can't remember where the rest of the Newport Girls were, but they were all somewhere other than Newport. Thus Rocky became my life away from home. My father had a double fit: Rocky had a sister who was a nun, and a lovely mother who would cook dinner for us every Sunday and tell me that "being Catholic is so wonderful." As much as I loved Rocky—he was my first true love—I knew he would never leave the Island, and I knew my destiny was somewhere else, so at about eighteen and a half, I left for the big city of Boston and decided that when I was old enough, I'd be an airline stewardess.

I went straight to Bonwit Teller (the most exclusive ladies' store in town in 1959) and asked if I could work there until I was old enough to apply to the airlines. The first one that hired me, I thought, I was on board. They said yes, and for a year and a half, I was the youngest lady to work in the robe department at Bonwit's, and for that matter, the youngest girl they had ever hired.

I lost track of the Newport Girls for several years—I was on a mission to make something of my life. I don't even remember if I ever went back those few years, because I had a plan, and going home would not "forward the action." I was right—Rocky never did leave Newport and I understand that at the age of eighty, he still asks for me when he sees some of the girls, who also never left.

My airline career was very cool and very short lived. American Airlines hired me and told us that five hundred women had applied for each of our jobs, and we were the chosen ones. *Wow.* I could have flown on my own wings to Fort Worth, Texas, where stewardess school was. There was only one fly in the ointment: I had met a gorgeous, very sophisticated twenty-nine-year-old man in Boston who'd swept me off my feet, literally, and he was not keen on my being a stewardess. I'll never forget Valentine's Day, 1961, He called me in Texas to tell me he loved me and wanted me to come home and get married. This was not cool, because in those days, you could not fly and be married.

I loved him, and I loved his mother and his stable home, and he was Jewish and a Harvard graduate. What's not to like here? But I just had to experience flying. So I graduated from stewardess school, got assigned to Boston, and flew for as long as I could before he said, "Me or the plane." It had to be him; I loved his mother too much. We got married by the justice of the peace, Ross Hamilton Currier on Gloucester Street, Boston, on April 21, 1961. Good old Ross was in his socks, and I'd just flown in from one of my three-day trips. My husband-to-be's youngest brother came down from college to stand up for him. I had no one; it was surreal. I think I flew for another week and then became Mrs. G.

Marriage #1

We really did have a fun beginning. We lived over the Darbury Room on Dartmouth Street, Boston, and we had a wedding party there. I think some of the Newport Girls came, but none of them were married yet, so from that point on, I was in another world. Mr. G's mother wanted me to have a lavish wedding party at her club, so I could get all the stuff brides are supposed to have. Not having a mother to guide me, I said "yes" to everything, and will be filled with love forever that she wanted me to have some of the trimmings of being married.

Leenie married her high school sweetheart, and I was in her wedding as a bridesmaid. Mr. G wouldn't come; in fact he made it very clear that my friends were from the past, and since he was nine years older than I, he had nothing in common with them. Therefore, *his* friends would be our friends. I caved, because he had "all the power," and I worked on being a good wife and eventually, over the years, the mother of two great boys (who today are truly my pride and joy—they have grown into pretty great men).

Fast-forward eight years. All the drama that led up to our divorce is not worth telling, but we did end our marriage, and until I was about thirty-seven, I was a working, struggling single mom. Life was hard for me and twice as hard for my boys. We didn't have much, but I made sure the boys had all the things they needed to grow up well, and their father agreed to all of it in the divorce agreement: braces, camp, college, etc., things I knew I might not ever be able to pay for. At thirteen, my oldest son wanted to go live with his father, and because his dad had remarried, he agreed. It was one of the first really painful decisions I had to make on behalf of my children.

The one constant in my life, through all those difficult years was "Mother G." It was very clear that *she* was the reason I'd married her son, and although I no longer wanted him as my husband, I still wanted her "as my adult mother." Incredible as she was, she never abandoned me, and until the day she died, forty years later, she was the mother I'd never had. I loved her beyond words.

After Mr. G re-married, I had no intention of being "the former Mrs.G," and one summer, I spent a lot of time back in Newport, reconnecting with whoever was still there. I tried not to be a "third wheel" in my old girlfriends' life. Judy had married Bob and lived in Portsmouth; Marianne had married Jack; Leenie had married Mack; Ginny had married Jack; Nancy had married Brian. I think Gretchen and Ellen had married Navy officers and were in other parts of the world. So I'd stay with Leenie or Judy, and even though I was "the odd man out," they were still the girls of my youth and I was so blessed to have them.

Marriage #2

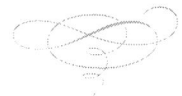

I can't remember when Leenie and Mack got divorced, but right after I married my second husband (my first "mid-life crisis") and moved to Virginia with my youngest son, Leenie and her two girls moved to Virginia as well, to live with her sister and family until she could get settled and start over, too.

Her second marriage was far more important than mine, because she has been married to Will for over twenty-three years, while my marriage was over in seventeen months: "My Lord," you are probably saying. "What were you thinking?" What I was thinking was, *how do I get out of Boston with no money?* One of the Newport Girls introduced me to a fine Washington attorney, and it looked like a plan to me. It did get me out of town; my only regret is the trauma it might have done to my youngest son. I hope he has forgiven me after all these years.

So, here I was again, divorced and a single parent and struggling. Do you see a pattern here? The most powerful experience of that short-lived marriage was my participating in the EST Training, what many people called brainwashing back in the seventies. To this day, it was some of the most powerful training of my life. The course no longer exists, and the current program, the Landmark Forum, has very little of the conversation we had in the EST Training. I did get one very important message from that training, and as a result, I cleaned up my life with my father.

I had always blamed my father for my mother being the way she was. She had walked out on us for good when I was seventeen, but she had followed me around until I lost her when I moved to Virginia. I don't know if I told Leenie that I'd done this until many years later; we never discussed our parents much. When I reconnected with my father, he and I cried for three days. With the realization that he had done the best he could, we forgave each other for all of the past. My father lived another ten years, and I can honestly say I ended up truly loving my father and allowed myself to finally be his little girl, and him to be my daddy.

Leenie's parents died first; that was my first experience of any of us being orphaned. Arlene and her sister were very good to their parents right up to the end, and I remember going to Betty's house for a memorial for one of them. She and Leenie would always joke about having a "Manhattan" (cocktail) for Rich—that was their dad. It had no meaning to me then, but perhaps it had great meaning to Arlene.

Over the next eight years, I was single again, but with a child to rear, it was hardly "being single." When my youngest was fifteen, he too said he wanted to go back to Boston and live with his father. Who was I to say no? He had every right to be with his dad, so off he went, when I was forty. For the first time in twenty years, I truly was single again.

I turned into a "wild child," having all kinds of experiences that did *not* require having money—I really felt like I had an exciting life. For five years, this was my life—until I met husband number three. Now—what didn't I get here?

I guess I was tired of having to struggle for so long, and this guy said he'd take care of me. Boy, did that sound good. So what's a girl to do? Get married!

Marriage #3

On July 4, 1986, "here I went again." I didn't even ask my boys to come. They were so disappointed by this point in my past behaviors regarding marriage that I was afraid if I invited them, they wouldn't even show up. So in front of a very few friends; we got married. I paid for the wedding—that should have been a clue of what was to come. The only Newport Girl to be there was Leenie (she had been to my second wedding too), and thus began another saga of my life: twelve years of living in complete irresponsibility, with my head up my ass. I gave my life over to Mr. C, because "he was going to take care of me."

I had no interest in anything other than finally having a "happy marriage." We had family holidays at our house. My oldest son had married his first wife, and we loved our daughter-in-law and her mom and were happy to share whatever time we could with them. We lived in Baltimore; they lived in Boston. My younger son lived in Los Angeles and had a darling girlfriend, and they came from time to time to share a Thanksgiving. I almost felt like I had a "normal life." Then my youngest son came back to New York and over the years found a stable work life and the girl who would become his bride and the mother of my three precious grandchildren.

Through all of this family fantasy, Leenie and her husband Will were always there for me. Leenie had no idea how miserable I was; but after three years of marriage, I knew I'd made another "marriage mistake." I was so consumed with guilt, I stayed married for nine more years, and because I was too ashamed to admit I'd made another wrong choice, I went into therapy, went through menopause (miserably, I might add), and even went to modeling school and had some face work done—anything to escape from the road I'd chosen for my life.

It needs to be said: I married three good men. When people ask me, "How many husbands have you had?" I say, "Fewer than Elizabeth Taylor and more than most women." Number one was the "man of my dreams," my fairytale man (who never loved me, by the way), but that marriage gave me two beautiful children and a mother I never had. There was one time she wanted to adopt me, even though both my parents were still alive. I was about thirty. How sweet was that?

Husband number two served a very important purpose: He got me out of Boston. I made a huge mistake. I never loved him.

Husband number three was to be "the charm." Everyone loved him, he loved me, and I really loved him—for the first three years. I don't want to say he was a fraud; it was more like he was totally inept at managing his own life, let alone being able to take care of mine. After twelve years of this mess (mostly financial), I knew I had to "call it quits" once more. There were bankruptcies (his, mine, and his business); our house was going into foreclosure, and the pain of it all was too much to handle any more. He was so devastated that I was leaving that I left my two precious dogs with him to care for. I knew he would love them as much as I did, and I could barely take care of myself at that point. It was the second most painful decision I ever had to make in my life; letting my children go to live with their father was the most painful.

He somehow kept the house, and I guess he has rebuilt his life (it's been over twelve years since I left). He did take wonderful care of my "babies" until they left this world to go to "doggy heaven" with Buttons, I hope.

My first husband also remarried. I hope he has been happy with his second wife for over thirty years. My sons have stayed close to their stepsiblings, and all of them seem to be happy. My second husband was a "blur on the screen of my life." I haven't a clue what has happened in his life since we parted. My youngest son said he "Googled" him once and found him in Maine. For me, he just served a purpose.

Needless to say, Leenie (and my kids) had just about had it with me and my marriages. Let's say I hold the distinction of being the "divorce queen" of the Newport Girls, and I swore to all of them I would never get married again!

Through these years, from twenty to fifty, we "girls" shared some unbelievable events that life never trains you for. Even if there was a manual on how to grieve for your friend's child's death, no one could grasp the enormity of that loss and the feeling of helplessness in comforting your friend. I don't know where I was when Mary and Bill's daughter died, but Leenie and I drove to Newport for the funeral of Ginny and Jack's son, who had also died. There are no words to express the grief and sorrow of sharing this unimaginable event, but we girls were all there, and I hope Ginny knows how deep our pain was for her. Gretch was our first and only widow. I think her Dick died around the age of fifty-one, and I know I was not there for her.

She was in California and we'd drifted apart for some time. When she came to Washington sometime later to visit, I was in awe of her strength, love, courage, and commitment not to let Dick's death define the happiness she might create for the rest of her and her sons' lives. She was the strongest woman I'd ever met, and she was grateful to have had him in her life for as long as she did. She was my hero. What a woman.

Healing

In 1988, I left my dogs and Baltimore and began "the next journey" of my journey. There are times I really feel like a cat that has nine lives, and for sure, I've not used them all up yet. My job (besides what I did to earn money) was to heal and nurture myself and only have lovely and loving women in my life as a support system. I found a tiny little apartment in the Maryland suburbs of Washington; I was so lucky to do this before the bankruptcy. Arlene and Will were living on Kent Island, about an hour away, and she came and made cushions for my chairs and curtains (she is a great seamstress and would bring her machine) and helped me make a "home for one" that was cozy and mine, and not cluttered with anything that would bring back bad memories. Leenie was always there when I needed her. We never stood on ceremony; no matter how long it had been since we'd seen each other, it always felt like she was no further than a phone call away.

Turning Fifty

I guess I have to say a little about the year we all turned fifty. That summer, we Newport Girls reunited for the first time in thirty-two years. The girls who'd stayed on the island always saw each other, but those of us who had moved away had never really been with *everyone* since we'd left Rogers High. It was a spectacular gathering in Ginny and Jack's backyard, a lovely event. Ginny's daughter helped serve food, and some of us brought our husbands. My experience is that it was a "social" rather than reuniting event, and that was fine, so different from what happened in June 2009.

I remember not feeling terribly connected to many of the girls; yes, Leenie, Gretch, Judy, and Mary had been my closest friends over the years, but I felt a kind of "disconnect" from the rest. After all, I was there with my third husband, and that made me extreme; most of these gals had only been married once. Only two had been married twice, and I felt "different" and somewhat unstable compared to the rest of them.

A bizarre thing occurred that evening in Ginny's backyard. Her yard backed up to Rocky's backyard (can you believe?), and he and I met in the bushes to say hello. We hadn't seen each other for decades, and it was one of the weirdest experiences I think I'd ever had. I had no feelings for him whatsoever—it would have been more bizarre if I had—and it felt almost "out of body" that I even agreed to do it. He came out of the trees, said hello to everyone, met my husband, and then went home. To this day, I wonder what his wife thought was going on.

Well, that was the last time all of the Newport Girls got together until June 2009.

Elaine Colton

The Newport Girls Turn Fifty

The Flower Girls

Turning Fifty

Leenie Turns Fifty

The Newport Girls

Marianne's Fiftieth Birthday Party

Friends Do the Darndest Things

The year was 1991, and my oldest son was planning his wedding with his first wife. As the mother of the groom, I had very little input into the wedding, but I was kind of excited when he and his bride-to-be chose to be married on the beautiful island of St. John, in the Virgin Islands. I can't remember why they chose this, and I was sad that Mother G and Papa could not attend (I think it was just too difficult a trip at their stage of life), but it sounded romantic: a beach wedding, and it truly was going to be a fabulous event.

I got to invite whomever I wanted, and given the distance and the cost of getting there and back, I wasn't too disappointed when most of the girls I invited said no, they just couldn't come. I had one friend from Washington who said yes, and I was thrilled to have at least one friend there with me to celebrate the wedding.

Leenie was still working, and we met one day for lunch in Washington, DC. She sadly told me there was no way she could be there because she had already made plans to do some sort of boating trip, and they couldn't change anything. I remember lamenting to Arlene that this was such an important event for me that I was quite devastated that she couldn't be there to share it with me.

Well, the day of the wedding arrived, and I was teary-eyed as my son and his bride were saying their vows on the sand. I was sobbing and missing my best friend, sad that she was not with me to witness this. The ceremony was over and we'd gathered with the other guests to eat and make toasts—all the stuff one does at a wedding. All of a sudden, I heard a chorus of "Elaine, Elaine!" I turned around, and who walked out of the ocean wearing their sarongs and condom earrings? Leenie, Gretch, and Leenie's sister Betty.

To say I almost fainted would be an understatement. My son said it was one of the highlights of his wedding! Here's how they pulled it off:

First, when Leenie and I had lunch that day, she knew they were sailing into St. John the day of the wedding, but, because they had no idea whether or not they could get an anchor spot for the boat when they arrived, she didn't want me to get my hopes up. They may not have been able to get in close enough and then I would be disappointed, so she kept all of that a secret and just said she couldn't come. They had been planning this all along. What a secret. So the day of the wedding, they all got into a dinghy and motored in to the beach (there were other people from the boat who were with them as well). They wanted to plan their arrival to occur after the ceremony so they wouldn't disrupt the wedding. Well, the picture speaks for itself—I was totally astonished. It is, to this day, one of the best surprises of my life.

They joined the guests and got a little "hammered," and when dusk fell and they were to return via dinghy to the boat, they asked me to come. Of course I said I couldn't; after all, I was the mother of the groom and it would have been in such poor taste to leave my son's wedding. So off they went. What a grand thing that I did not go back with them. Upon arriving back at the sail boat (so Leenie tells me), one of the girls stood up to disembark and capsized the dinghy and all of them with it! No one was hurt, thank goodness, but boy oh boy, am I glad I wasn't there; I'd have had some kind of explaining to do!

I can honestly say this was probably the BEST surprise I'd ever had in my life, up to that moment.

The Girls Surprise Me in St. John

Great Friends Forever

The Newport Girls

Everyone Just Keeps "Getting Better"

Year 2000

The best part of my life began in the year 2000 and continues today.

From 1998 to 2000, I lived a very quiet life of work and great friendships with women. Aside from Leenie, none of these women were Newport Girls. They were wonderful women I'd met and embraced through work and professional associations, and I was very blessed to include younger women (in their thirties), older women (in their sixties), and my own contemporaries in this group. We had a powerful connection: mutual love, respect, and appreciation for each other; each one held her own special place in my heart—and still does.

During these two years, wonderful and challenging events took place: my divorce from Mr. C, my youngest son's marriage, my bankruptcy and all the roadblocks that presents, and maybe the most important personal experience: I healed and was perfectly content to live a quiet, simple, happy life alone, without the need for anyone else to take over responsibility for my life. I had finally stepped up to the plate and embraced being alone, on my own, and it truly was a celebration. I now know that for my whole life, I'd been searching and yearning for someone to take care of me, because I guess I'd felt I'd always been taking care of the whole world.

Life shifted, and I was very content, happy, and at peace, and I needed nothing. Perhaps one truly has to get to that space of total self-contentment before one is available for what I call "personal miracles" to occur for no reason.

The Love of My Life

It was March 2000, and I was working a trade show at the DC Convention Center. A very charming man, whom I'd known professionally for about ten years, came up to our booth to chat with my coworker. Somehow, I intruded, and without going into all the embarrassing events, two months later he invited me out to dinner. As they say, "That's all they wrote." We just must have been the right people for each other, and we've been together ever since.

We are blessed with four adult children, their three spouses (one divorce, unfortunately), and five absolutely awesome grandchildren. They all seem to be happy that we are together, and for the first time in my life, I have committed to forever and really mean it. We've had a lot of marriages between us, and we see no need to repeat that step. We both love each other dearly and intend to be each other's partner for as long as the gift of life affords us. I truly did save the best for last.

2009

So it is coming up to June of 2009, and life is going fairly well. I hate the fact that I'm still working, because I am so ready to be free from that rat race and begin the next phase of life. Rick (my sweetie) bought a darling little house for us in North Carolina, and I'm very anxious to move and enjoy a slower way of life. Rick is the CEO and president of a company in Virginia, and he is energized every day he goes to work. I am very excited that he has said we will be in North Carolina by the middle of 2011, so I know I can be very content with our Washington life until then. Leenie and Will will live about thirty-five miles from us, in Southport, North Carolina, so in my final golden years, my dearest friend will live practically in my backyard. Leenie tells me to get there soon, before I'm too old to unpack the boxes (I keep reminding Rick we're not thirty anymore). Leenie and Will have been in North Carolina for about four years and have really created a new life there. Aside from being jealous that she's way ahead of me, I am so happy for her.

Leenie and Will are driving to Newport in late June for a cousin's wedding, and apparently, some of the Newport Girls are coming back and will be there. Gretch is there for her month in Newport, in her condo, and Leenie wants me to come.

I really don't want to go; somewhere in my head is the idea that I don't mean anything to these girls. Why bother? After all, it was they who made the difference to me, not the other way around, and I truly felt so disconnected from most of them. My initial response is no.

I need to say that I never went to any of our high school reunions; I'm not one who likes to look back. Anyway, who wants to see that all those cute boys from my youth have turned fat, bald, and ugly? The truth is I have no idea how they turned out, because in high school the boys were way down on my list of who was important in my life; it was always the Newport Girls that I cared about. This was the year of our fiftieth high school reunion, and I absolutely was not going to that, either—but maybe seeing "the girls" would be a good idea; after all, it had been eighteen years since I'd seen some of them.

So after some thought, and encouragement from my Rick, I told Leenie okay, I would go. Leenie and Will were driving up from North Carolina and stopping along the way to visit friends, so it didn't really work for them to pick me up in Maryland. That was not a problem for me; Rick said he'd treat me to the airfare into Providence, and I could rent a car and drive to Newport. Over the years, Mary and Bill Clark had graciously allowed me to stay with them in their precious home in Portsmouth, so I called Mary and asked if I could stay and she said yes.

Mary was organizing a dinner for all the girls for one night, and I would arrive the day before. Leenie would be there, Gretch was there from San Diego, Lynn was coming in from Iowa, Barbara was there from Little Compton, RI, Eileen was coming from New Hampshire, and Ellen was coming from Florida. Mary, Ginny, Marianne, and Nancy, the local gals, were already there, of course. I had called Judy in Michigan and asked her to come, but she'd been back that Easter, and the time did not work for her. She was the only Newport Girl really missing for me, even though it would have been fun to see Kathy, Sally, and Linda. It had been so many years since I'd seen most of them that I was just excited to be with those who would be there.

One of the reasons I said I'd go was that Leenie told me about a girl we'd known in high school who was in Newport and was dying of a brain tumor. Leenie said that Helen had always asked for me, and even though she was not part of our gang, something told me to go and see her. When I arrived that first day, Mary and I visited her in the nursing home, and I'm so glad we did. It had been fifty years since I'd seen her. Given her medical condition, there was no space to trivialize over the past fifty years of our lives, but we spent a half hour discussing the *now*.

Helen's impending death brought me face-to-face with how fragile and unpredictable life is. Oprah always says, "Live your best life." None of us has a clue how long this life on earth will be. I thought about the deaths of my own mother and father; they were both gone, and as an orphan myself, reflection on so much loss came welling up in my visit with Helen. I'd now lost three mothers—my real mother, my aunt who sent me away, and Mother G. Now there clearly are several ways to spin this; I chose this one: How blessed was I to have had three mothers. Helen died the following winter.

So, back to Newport and the impending excitement of seeing all the girls once more. As I told you at the beginning, I felt an astonishing amount of emotion as I traveled over the Newport Bridge from Jamestown.

So many of my prior trips here had been for some kind of escape, but this time, there was something welling up that would reveal itself as the days went on. In the past, I'd cried for my lost youth, for all my wrong choices, for all my failures. But this trip was different. It wasn't until visiting with Mary, Gretch, Leenie, Ginny, Marianne, Barbara, Eileen, Lynn, Nancy and Ellen that I got the true purpose of this trip: to celebrate the joy of being in each other's lives, on and off, for over half a century.

Mary and Me

It began anew when I called Mary from the parking lot of the Newport Creamery to say I was making a pit stop along the way. She said to come get her, and we'd go together. I *needed* a Creamery cheeseburger and a frappe (I think they call them milkshakes in DC, but they are frappes in Rhode Island). Pulling into Mary's driveway brought back so many memories.

Mary is truly wonderful; we have just been friends forever. She and Bill have been together for over forty years. Mary was a nurse and Bill had been an executive with Mobil Oil. They had adopted two daughters (I knew neither of these children). They endured the unimaginable loss of Courtney, their child, but through all their trials, tribulations, and excruciating sorrow, they have been married for forty-five years. I love Mary and Bill.

Mary and I hadn't seen each other for a while, but you know how some people never change? Mary is one of those people. She looked fabulous, and when I finally saw Bill, later in the day, he looked amazing, too. We are all so blessed. As I will tell you again later in this tale, all the Newport Girls looked amazing. Just as with Leenie and Gretch, being with Mary seemed as if I'd seen her just the other day; and it had actually been years. Some friendships have no time, space, or boundaries associated with them. My friendship with Mary seems to be one of those. We never discussed the drama of our lives and yet we always seemed to be connected.

Well, off to the Newport Creamery. Remember, I had been a "head scooper" there fifty years ago, and I guess my memories went back to my teenage experience. What an extreme disappointment. The cheeseburger was underwhelming, and the frappe was a weak concoction. It might just have been a bad day at the Newport Creamery. Who knows? But for me, in the moment, I was truly "over" the Newport Creamery—for that trip, anyway!

Gretchen has owned a condo in Newport for years, and she comes for a month, every year, from San Diego. She sees who she wants to see in Newport and always visits her huge family for a reunion in New Hampshire. I think Gretch was a very wise businesswoman and after Dick's death made some very prudent real estate investments. I was very excited that my first night in town, Gretch had invited Mary, Ellen, and me to dinner. I only remember Gretchen as a bubbly, happy-go-lucky girl and woman—and smart. I hadn't seen Gretchen in fifteen years.

When Mary and I got to Gretch's that evening, all I could see was the Gretch I'd always known and loved; I loved her as much as I did when we were kids. She is a "hoot" and she had a surprise waiting for me: Leenie and Will were there for a few minutes, just long enough for me to be ecstatic, give them a hug, and take some pictures. Then they were on their way to something they had planned.

Now Leenie has been an amazing craftsperson all her adult life, and her latest adventure is making and decorating miniature houses for inside use. She had brought one for Gretch that she had made: a replica of Gretch's condo, complete with flip-flops and sand. It lit up, too; it was just adorable. That Leenie—what a girl. She and Will stayed with Marianne and Russ, and she brought them one, too. She is amazing.

Gretchen and Me

Now I must tell you how Gretchen and I have stayed connected over the past several years: it's been through movies! We both love them and she was Nana West, I was Mid-Atlantic Nana, and Leenie was Nana Southeast. NW and NMA would send movie reviews to each other every time we saw one, good or bad, but mostly good. Gretch likes foreign movies; I can't stand subtitles; except for *Crouching Tiger*, which I loved so much that the subtitles were no problem for me. So Gretch and I had planned to go see a movie together while we were in Newport. I was so excited to share popcorn with my three-thousand-mile movie buddy. I looked forward to it so much, along with the beach, but we'll get to the beach later. So back to dinner at Gretch's. It was delicious; we laughed, we drank wine. Ellen was a delight, not as boisterous as the rest of us, but who cared? We were all together. Now this group goes to bed early, so by 10:00 PM, Gretch shooed us out and that was okay, because the next night was the big dinner with the whole gang (all that were there anyway).

A quick word about the weather: it sucked. Having lived in the Washington DC area for thirty years, I truly had forgotten how unpredictable Newport weather could be in June. I was so spoiled. I'd been going to the beach in Rehoboth, Delaware since May, so freezing, yucky, rainy weather was a shock. The day of our dinner, Mary and I planned to meet Marianne, Leenie, and Gretch for lunch, after we visited Marianne's daughter Stacy's darling ladies' boutique. I only remembered Stacy as a little girl, and as a grown woman, she was delightful. I'll tell you about Marianne in a bit.

Elaine Colton

Well Stacy's store was adorable, and I was grateful that she had a great coat in my size and I stimulated the Newport economy that day. I never took that coat off until I got home the following Sunday. I was so glad I'd brought knee socks and jeans; I felt like I was dressed for March, not June.

Marianne

Marianne looks amazing; I know I'm throwing superlatives around in here, but it's no exaggeration. As you see who we were then and see how we are now, you will find it hard to disagree—these women are awesome. Marianne has never changed. Maybe it's good genes, maybe it's being happy, maybe it's good husbands, maybe it's good children, maybe it's the good Newport Island experience, or maybe it's all of it. I hadn't seen Marianne since we were fifty, and she is a wonder. Now I may be a liar here, but I don't think any of these girls have had work done on their faces—except me! Leenie had her eyelids done a year ago, because she was beginning to lose some sight, but hers was truly a medical, not a vanity issue, and yes, Leenie looks terrific too, but it's not just her eyes. I'll tell you more about her later.

Marianne married Jack when she was twenty-something and had two children by him. I don't know the details of the split, or I can't remember, but Marianne ended her marriage after eight years. When she found Russ eludes me as well; but like Leenie, she found her true love, and they have been happily married for thirty-five years.

It's very clear to see that each of us has traveled a different path, but the common bond was always *us* and Newport. Marianne is a successful realtor, knows everyone, and is a true Newporter for life. I am so happy she is in my life.

Ginny

Ginny and I reconnected that night at our reunion dinner. We had been out of touch for years. After her son died, she retreated and most likely only stayed close to her most intimate friends. I never was mad about this, because I can't even begin to know how broken your heart gets, or if it ever truly heals, after your child is gone. This is not the way life is supposed to go—no one should ever have to bury her child.

So it had been eighteen years since Ginny and I had seen each other on a happy occasion, and my love for her hadn't waned one bit. I don't know how long Ginny has been married to Jack, but the bond they share, just like the bond Mary and Bill share, as parents who lost their child, is something none of us can even begin to grasp. As they say, that which doesn't kill you makes you stronger. They are still together after all these years. If memory serves me right, Ginny was a teacher and Jack was principal of one of the Middletown schools, and they have lived right in Newport for years. At dinner that evening, Ginny reminisced about her trips to visit me in Boston, before I became a stewardess, with such pleasure. She said I'd been a really good friend. Funny how we remember only what we want—I didn't remember much of those times, but I was so happy to hear her talk of good times we shared together.

Turning Fifty
More to Say about That

MEMORIES: The year was 1991 and Leenie and I, and for that matter all the girls, were turning fifty. It was a pivotal time in my life for many reasons. First and foremost, I had lost my mother. In spite of her mental incapacities, my mother was tenacious; when I flew for American Airlines, somehow she found out and wrote to the president of the airlines to find out what he'd done to her daughter. It was more than mortifying. She found out I'd gotten married, and she found me in Boston and followed me around all the time. It was a nightmare. She embarrassed me on my jobs, she harassed me on the phone, and I could never escape her, as hard as I tried. I made some very tough decisions in those days about my mother, and when I got pregnant at age twenty-one, I vowed no child of mine would be exposed to this dreadful woman. Was it the right thing to do? Maybe not, but I felt I owed it to my children to have only loving people in their lives, and my mother was so unstable, I just wasn't about to chance it. So, by some miracle, I eluded my mother for many years and my children never knew her.

I think I regret that decision. As adults, my sons were capable of understanding my mother's illness and might have had some connection with her. I do remember my oldest son visiting her with me once when he lived in Boston and she was in her first nursing home. My reasoning was that Mother G was such a loving, powerful influence in their lives that I wanted them to experience nothing less from a grandmother. Good or bad, I decided, and they never really wanted to know my mother—that was fine with me.

When I remarried and moved to Baltimore, somehow she found me again. That time, my kids were grown up and on their own, and I could handle her from afar. I even went to visit her with my third husband once in Boston; it was manageable. So for years she'd call on my birthday and we'd share some inane conversations, and that would be that. This year (1991), something changed. There was no call from my Mother. At first it was not a big deal, but as days passed by I found myself beginning to worry; I had never worried about her before in my life. Where was my mother? Had something happened to her? I was actually suffering from the worry and I called the Boston Police and asked for their help. Could they find my mother?

Some days you're just lucky, and I got the most wonderful, understanding cop on the phone, and he took over from there. I can't remember where they found my mother, but they did, and she was alive and in a hospital. I flew to Boston to once and forever take care of my mother; for you see, in those two or three days while I waited in fear of the worst, I discovered the most amazing thing: I truly loved my mother. I vowed that if they found her, I would take care of her for the rest of her life and finally become the daughter I never knew how to be.

My mother was very ill, but was diagnosed as well as one with her conditions could be, and with the help of a wonderful social worker, we found a loving nursing home for her in Boston and I returned to Baltimore, knowing she would no longer be in harm's way.

I thought about bringing her to Baltimore so I could be closer, but with good counsel, I decided to leave her in Massachusetts, because they have one of the best healthcare systems available for mentally ill people. I can truly say that for the last thirteen years of her life, she was well taken care of.

Now for another fabulous event of my fiftieth year: Aside from our reunion with all the girls, Leenie and I made a separate trip to Newport to celebrate Marianne's birthday. We drove up from Maryland and had a great girls' long weekend. Marianne's party was great, and lots of the girls were there.

One of the highlights of that trip was that Leenie and I "relived our youth." We started on Jude Street, where we'd met. The drive-in was gone; that was very sad for me. We headed out for the Creamery, visited all the schools we'd gone to together, and finally ended up at Third Beach, which held so many wonderful memories of our teenage years. Leenie will tell you more about Third Beach in a bit.

My Mom and Me
The Final Chapter

It was August of 2005 and Rick and I were flying in to Boston for my dear friend Judee's only daughter's wedding. This was very special to me. Leslee and my oldest son had been born the same year, and Judee and I met as new, young mothers. We have been friends ever since. Both my boys and Leslee ended up going to the same camp for years. So this was special.

I said to Rick, "I want to see my mother on this trip." The nursing home had called and said my mother wasn't doing too well, and since she was in the suburbs of Boston, it made perfect sense to me to visit her, too—and say "good-bye" in person and be completely complete. Rick was concerned this would upset me, but to the contrary, had I not seen my mom, I think I would have been so angry with myself in the future. So trusting in my courage, the morning of the wedding, we rented a car and drove to the nursing home. I had called ahead to tell the nurses I was coming, and they told me not to expect too much. I expected nothing.

When we arrived, the nurses had moved my mother to a private room with lots of sunlight. Mom looked beautiful, and amazingly young to me. Maybe when you don't have a normal brain, you have no stress or worries and your face doesn't reflect the wear and tear of aging. Rick was very gentle and took a seat at the back of the room. The nurse left, saying that my mother could no longer speak and she knew no one. I went to the side of her bed and took her hand, and said, "Hi, Mama. It's Elaine." I told her how beautiful she looked and how happy I was to see her. She started to cry—she must have known it was me.

I started to cry gently; I was crying for all the life we'd not been able to share together. I was crying because I loved my mother so much. I was crying because I knew I was saying good-bye. I told her she could go anytime she was ready, and I was okay with that. And then we left, and that was that.

The months of September, October, and November went by, and I kept calling the nursing home to see what was going on with my mom. The nurses said it was a total mystery. People were dying all around her, and she was rallying. It was very apparent to me; she was just not ready to go. And then one day it came, the call I knew I'd hear soon enough; my mom had passed away. I think it was about the fifth of December; the date is not important. She was gone. I cried for my youth, for *all* my mothers, and for the experience of being a middle-aged orphan. It was lonely.

Then I got on with it. Many years before, before my uncle died (he was my mother's youngest brother) and I became my mother's legal guardian, we had made complete arrangements for this day. My mom would be taken care of once again.

Thanksgiving was over. We celebrate Christmas and Chanukah in our home, so I just plunged into getting our home festive for the upcoming holidays—and waiting for my mother to "arrive." She was being cremated and then being sent to me. Well, our home was wonderful and we were planning for Rick's kids and grandkids to come for Christmas, and I kept wondering, *Where's my Mother?*. Having never gone through this before, I had no idea how long the process was, so I kept anticipating her arrival.

At one time I asked Rick if he thought my mother had gotten lost in the holiday mail, because, I learned, you can only transport remains by the United States Postal Service—so no Fed Ex for my mom. I'd just have to be patient.

Rick's girls had sent me beautiful white roses, and I so appreciated their compassion as we celebrated Christmas Eve. The day after Christmas, I was finally cleaning up and there was a knock at my front door. I could see my wonderful mail lady with our mail and a package in brown paper.

I opened the door and said, "Becky, I'm so excited to see you. You have my mother." She sort of cringed, and I said, "I can't think of anyone I'd rather have my mom ride around with than you!" I signed for the package and Becky left. *Now what?*

I'd had two thoughts about where I wanted to leave my mom; one was the beach I so dearly loved and had spent so many glorious days at for over thirty years. The other was the Potomac. I used to pass the Potomac River every day as I headed into Washington on my way to work. I finally chose the Potomac, and I knew just the perfect spot! Did I tell you that once my mother arrived, I stuck her in my home office closet because I hadn't decided when the final event would take place? I finally asked Rick if I could drop my mother off in the Reflecting Pool in front of the Capitol. He said, "No, the water doesn't circulate in the Reflecting Pool." So it was going to be plan number two.

Now, one is not allowed to drop remains into the Potomac, so this was to be a "covert operation." I asked Rick if he'd come with me, and my love said yes and the plan was in action. It was to take place New Year's Eve morning, before dawn, when no one (like the Park Police) could see us. I thought it was totally appropriate to end the year with a final farewell and create the space for a joyous beginning of a new year. Rick is far more concerned about "doing what is correct" than I am, but there was not an ounce of hesitation on his part to be my partner in what was, for me, an event.

So, New Year's Eve morning, in the pitch dark, I got up—it was hardly a surprise that I couldn't sleep, so very quietly, I put on some sweats and went to get my mom out of the closet. Rick was still asleep!

What is it about a plain brown wrapper? Conjure up anything? I'd remembered reading in the back of magazines I'd read at the library when I was a kid that certain things would be sent to you in a plain brown wrapper. This was not one of those things. The box was the size of a shoebox (small-size ladies' shoes), and it was so sealed unbelievably well. It took me about ten minutes just to open the paper. Then there was the box—well it was impossible to open the plastic box, but I had to open it. Reluctantly, I woke Rick up and asked if he'd help me get my mom out of the box. These are the moments when your love for someone is so deep that there are no words.

He rubbed his eyes, slowly sauntered into the kitchen, and opened the box—and then went to get dressed. We had no time to waste; the clock was ticking.

I opened the box, and there was my mother. *Oh yeah?* Let me tell you, these are the moments in life when, if you have any faith at all, it sure kicks in, because there was a baggie with some sand in it. It was very hard to wrap my arms around "this is my mother." But there was no time to ponder the ways of life; we had to move!

Rick had gotten a useless piece of glass that had come from Tiffany's from one of his vendors. I repurpose a lot of stuff and kept the box because I was sure that I'd use it again for something. I ran to get the box and stuck my mother in it—and it was perfect. I wanted to honor her properly, so I put some pretty pink tissue paper around her and two of the white roses the girls had sent. It truly was a lovely presentation. So off we went in the dark toward DC.

Rick said, "Where to"? And I said, "Just drive. I'll tell you when it's time to stop." My experience is that men don't like taking directions from women for anything, but you gotta love him. He just drove. When we got to the Lincoln Memorial, we had choices, but to get to the Potomac, there's only one way to go, so he turned right. I said, "Stop," and he parked.

There is a very short stretch of grass that leads up to the edge of the river, and that was where I wanted to finally let my mother go. I'd stopped there many times before to admire the beauty of the river and the awesomeness of the city, and to enjoy the planes flying overhead in and out of Reagan Airport. We went right to the edge; dawn was just breaking; we looked around—no one there but us. I opened the box and let the roses go. Rick opened the baggie of ashes, and I let my mother drift off into the peacefulness she very rarely experienced in her adult life. I think I said something like, "Have a more gentle life now than you had." I turned to Rick and said, "That's it," and he said, "That's it?" Yes—that was it. I'd dropped my mom off in the Potomac, and I was as at peace as I hoped she was.

We left the box in a trash container and laughed wondering whether anyone cleaning trash would think there was anything odd about seeing a beautiful Tiffany box in a Potomac trash bin. We went off to the Channel Inn to have breakfast, and we toasted my mom with orange juice and wished her a good afterlife. For me, it was a very fitting way to end the year.

Since then, at least once a week, I pass by. I think of Lincoln and his impact on the country, and I think about my mom, and who I turned out to be—good or bad—because she was my mother.

Back To 2009

I discovered an amazing thing when I reunited with the Newport Girls, this June of 2009; something that had never occurred to me in my entire life. These girls—now women—had so shaped the fiber of my life; and I knew how much they meant to me, but I never had any idea of what I might have meant to them.

It was something Mary said, so casually, that stopped me in my tracks. It was something like, "Well, dear (that's how Mary talks), you don't know what kind of a force you were in our lives." Well, damn straight; I had no idea that I had made any difference in any of their lives; after all, I was the one that needed *them*—they certainly did not need *me*! Finding out that they did was truly shocking to me.

Now, anyone who knows me knows I am very clear about the things I speak; nothing obscure or fuzzy ever comes out of this mouth. I am straight and direct and believe me, I have paid the price for being this way many a time in my life, but that's the path I've chosen—straight and direct. No one would ever have to say, "What did she mean by that?" But when Mary said I was such a "force" in their lives, I truly didn't have a clue what that meant. So I asked her, and her response was such a surprise to me.

Mary said I had been the bold one, the "out-of-the-box one," way before bold and out-of-the-box was cool. She said I was fearless. Maybe I'm exaggerating a little here, but the gist was, most of the Newport Girls had come from fine, quiet, traditional homes, and they were kind of led down the paths their lives would take them. I, on the other hand, seemed to steer my own ship (I'm paraphrasing here), and that was quite a force for everyone else in the group. To say I was surprised would have been an understatement. It was the first glimmer that I'd ever had that I had contributed to their lives in some small way. I was truly moved.

Gretch, Me, and the Movies

It would be safe to say that we have access to some mighty fine movie establishments in Washington DC. We have stadium theaters in Georgetown, Chinatown, and the suburbs of Maryland and Virginia, and Landmark Theatres about ten minutes from where we live; as far as movies go, we are spoiled.

Newport is another story. I know there was the Strand, the Opera House and the Paramount in downtown Newport when we were growing up. What fun to make out and kiss boys in the back row of the balcony on a Saturday matinee—where else did you learn how to kiss? But that was then and this is now, and although those theaters still exist in Newport, there is only one Cineplex on the Island. But Gretch and I were going to see an afternoon movie together, no matter what. We paid for movie number one and then snuck in to movie number two. We could have seen every damn movie in the joint—no one would have known or cared—but we laughed ourselves silly about seeing the second and sharing popcorn. It really was like being kids again.

Maybe when you have the pure joy of just being with your friend, you always feels like a kid. One more joyous moment in the hour of our lives.

Leenie and Me

The rest of the story is about Leenie and me. There are no two ways about it—no better friend has ever walked this earth than my friend Arlene.

When Will retired and Leenie stopped working, I was so jealous. They were so happy and were not burdened by the stress of day-to-day work; so it seemed to me, anyway. I always knew I could "live on nothing." Why? Because I had! So I never felt like I had to work forever to make enough money, because I always felt like I already had enough money.

So I watched Leenie and Will prepare to leave Kent Island and build a new retirement home in Southport, North Carolina, near her sister Betty and Betty's husband Tom. I wanted so badly to move right next door to her, but I am a realist, and my life with Rick is great. Soon enough we will be right down the road a piece.

We made several trips to visit them in their lovely home over the last several years, and while Will is building his airplane and riding his motorcycle, Leenie has made a beautiful home for them, made great friends, and enjoyed her crafts and the beach; she has paved the way for when we get there. My friend Leenie is bubbly, funny, kind, friendly, loyal, and loving. So when I got the call sometime after Thanksgiving, 2008, I nearly fainted.

Leenie said something like, "I want you to know I am an alcoholic and I've stopped drinking." I said to myself, *what do you mean an alcoholic? I've known you practically my entire life and I had absolutely no idea.* I know I said something inane like, "Wow, good for you," or something equally asinine, but all I could think was, *Oh my God, my best friend really is in trouble, and I can't help her.* So I did what I always do: tried to think of some way to make it better. I ran out and bought her a very cool day calendar so she could mark off each day she was sober and sent it to her—and then I just prayed, because if I can't fix it and I can't control it, I worry incessantly about the outcome. This was my best friend's life we're talking about here, and I was terrified and praying for her success.

It would be an understatement to say that this girl is beyond amazing. I can only imagine what it has been like in every social situation where alcohol abounds, but she has never wavered. Every day she's sober—over a year and a half now—my heart applauds her courage and bravery. She has battled cancer and won that one too, but this demon will follow her all the days of her life, and I know she will win this one, too. I can't wait to get to North Carolina and share iced tea with her, for the rest of our lives.

So the reunion came to an end, and some of the Newport Girls were looking forward to the Rogers High Fiftieth Reunion that would be coming up that July. My reunion had already occurred. I'd seen all the people I loved and cared about and came home inspired, renewed, and totally appreciative of these great women I have had in my life.

And so it goes. The Newport Girls rock on and who knows where this will end. The memories are here forever.

Mary, Gretch and Me—2009

Ginny and Me—2009

Nancy, Mary, and Eileen—2009

Leenie—2009

Eileen, Mary, Marianne, and Gretch—2009

Ellen, Barbara, and Lynn—2009

Gretch, Barbara, and Dottie—2009

Lynn and Marianne—2009

Arlene Callahan Dovel—My Story

It was June 19, 2009, and I was packing the car to prepare for a wonderful journey. I was driving to Newport, Rhode Island to attend a reunion with my girlfriends who graduated from high school with me fifty years ago. Although I was born and raised in Newport, this to me was a "first-time" trip because it would be the "first time" I would be celebrating a reunion with these wonderful friends while I was sober. Six months ago, I stopped drinking. My name is Leenie, and I am a recovering alcoholic.

In 1952, my parents moved us into a simple ranch house in Middletown, Rhode Island. My father worked for the government and had been transferred from Chicago back to our hometown, and I was very excited. There were four of us in my family: my mom, my dad, my sister Betty, and me. We also had a crazy dog named "Buttons." I was going into the sixth grade and my mother wanted to send me to a Catholic school in Newport. I believe that "things happen for a reason," and lo and behold, my friend, Elaine, came into my life for a very good reason. Over the summer, Elaine convinced my parents to let me attend the local grammar school, Berkeley Peckham, in Middletown. Needless to say, Elaine and I became the "dearest" of friends forever and ever. This was the beginning of an unconditional friendship that would last well into our golden years. Over the years, our lives would take us in different directions, but we would always find our way back to one another. We always said that we didn't "stand on ceremony," and when our paths crossed again, we would pick up where we left off—and we did.

The Newport Girls

Let me tell you about my friend, Elaine. She lived across the street from us with her dad and brother. Her father and my father used to carpool together to work. Elaine's mother had a serious mental illness and was committed to a mental hospital in Boston. Elaine had to grow up much too soon. She became the "mother" of this family at eleven years old. Elaine could do anything, from cooking the dinner at night to doing the laundry to grocery shopping. She was so sophisticated. She seemed to know everything about life. I was a shy, unworldly young girl who knew nothing about life, but she would soon teach me so much. I wanted to be just like her.

Elaine and I would lay a blanket down in my backyard and talk about our dream that we would be on Broadway someday. We even wrote a song called "You'll Get by if You Harmonize," and we sent it to Rodgers and Hammerstein in New York. We dreamed that they would like it enough to bring us to New York and let us sing it onstage in a play. Needless to say, we received a letter in the mail that rejected our song. That didn't stop us and we continued to dream every day on that blanket in my backyard. We would play with our Vogue dolls, but we would always go back to that dream.

As my husband and I crossed over the Newport Bridge on a not-so-sunny day, the memories of the past came rushing back. Could I handle this "first time" without slipping? I repeated the Serenity prayer over and over again. I prayed to my "Higher Power" to give me the strength to get through this. I wanted to enjoy this time with my girlfriends because I had not seen many of them in a few years. I was excited but I was so afraid.

We (the girlfriends) have endured so many sad times over the years. We have been there for one another through the deaths of husbands, divorces, children that died because they took their own lives, and cancer. With the grace of God, we are all still alive and well. This is amazing and truly a blessing.

As I was getting ready for our first dinner event, I wanted to look my very best. Not because I wanted to look like the "youngest" or the "prettiest," but because I felt so good and I looked better than I had ever looked because I'd stopped drinking. My face wasn't bloated anymore; my stomach wasn't sticking out because of all the booze. It was amazing what alcohol could do to your looks, your mental health, your physical being. Was I trying to prove something to myself? Yes, I certainly was. I was so damn proud of myself, I couldn't stand it. I wanted everyone to be just as proud of me. Yes, it was all about me. So, with my head held high and my chest sticking out with pride, I entered the room at the restaurant. Did any heads turn around and say, "Gee, Leenie, looks ten years younger, doesn't she? Gosh, Leenie certainly is prettier than any of us, isn't she? Boy, I wonder if she has had work done on her face."

All these things were going through my head. But at the end of the day, every one of my beautiful girlfriends in that room stood with their heads held high and their chests sticking out, and they were the most beautiful sight I have seen in my life. I felt the love in that room like I have never felt it before. You know what? It wasn't all about *me*—it was all about *us*.

Let's "rewind" back to the fifties. One of the most memorable times for the Newport Girls was the summertime and our beach days. There were days when a lot of the "good girls" would meet at the beaches, but then there were days when Elaine, Judy, and I would just go to the beach together. The name of the beach that was our favorite was Third Beach. You have got to "get" Newport. The beaches do have real names, but the Newporters named them according to the way you drove to them from Newport. There was "First Beach" (Easton's Beach), and then as you drove on, there was "Second Beach" (Sachuest Beach), and then there was "Third Beach" (Peabody's Beach). At one end of Third Beach sat the families and the "good girls," and at the far end of the beach, sat the "fast girls" and the "fast boats," where they would all go water skiing. We seldom visited the "far end," but would if we were "invited."

Back to the "good girls." This beach was special to us because it had our favorite food stand that Mrs. Peabody owned and ran. Have you ever heard of a "Frozen Charleston Chew"? Well, Mrs. P had them, and boy did they hit the spot when you were sitting in that afternoon sun. She also made the best hamburgers in town. She was such a character and hardly spoke a word, but you would hear from her if you didn't give her the right amount of change for your Charleston Chew! We would also order a soda, and when we took our bottles back, we got two cents back. Fast forward: When I took my daughters to Third Beach, they would get an Orange Crush, and when they returned the container, Mrs. Peabody would give them a package of Bazooka Bubble Gum.

Those were the days. Mrs. P was always "old" to us. She was adorned every day in a huge beach hat that tied under the chin. She walked with a crooked walk and wore a housedress that was very long and, of course, beach sandals. She lived in a house across from the beach. I believe it was her family that owned the rights to the beach. Needless to say, in our later years, we referred to the beach as "Mrs. Peabody's Beach."

Elaine, Judy, and I would just lie on that beach (again on that same blanket that came from my backyard) and talk about—what else? Boys! We even had our picture taken by the *Newport Daily News* and it appeared in the paper that summer. Third Beach was also the beach that my parents took me to when I was little to have swimming lessons. I remember how I hated to go into that water because it was so cold. Years later, Third Beach was also the beach I took *my* children to for their swimming lessons.

Third Beach is and always will be a big part of my childhood life, and remains important even in my golden years. When the Newport Girls all turned fifty, we met at Third Beach for an afternoon. Somehow, I will always be drawn back to that beach. I am hoping to visit that beach again with my two granddaughters in two years when I reach the "wistful" age of seventy. Hopefully, we will walk on that same silky sand, wade in that peaceful and gentle water, and make new footprints in the sand—that would be six footprints. We will also make new memories. Perhaps they will take their children to that beach someday and tell them about how their nana and mother grew up on that beach.

Gretchen Buxbaum Kelly—My Story

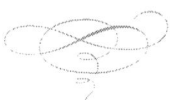

I was born on July 21, 1941 in Boston, Massachusetts and moved with my family to Newport, Rhode Island in 1954, where I started seventh grade at John Clark Junior High School. My family consisted of my mother, my father, and my younger brother, Pete. We lived for the first twelve years of my life in lovely homes in the suburbs of Boston, where my father was part owner of a very affluent, family-run, grocery store. I can still remember having our groceries delivered daily to our home. I also remember accompanying my grandfather as he shopped for meats, fruits, and vegetables throughout the city of Boston. I had years of lazy summers with my grandparents and cousins on Cape Cod, which resulted in a special family bond. One summer, our grandfather gave all of us pet ducks. They ran all over the thirteen acres of property while eating out of vegetable and fruit gardens. At the end of that summer, they were returned to their original owners. It was years later that we found out our job was to fatten them up for the holidays. Another memorable summer was when a real bathroom was installed. Until then, we'd used the outhouse and bathe in the pond that was part of the property. The memories of my family have given me great comfort over the years; we all remain very close to one another.

My parents separated and divorced when I was thirteen years old and we were living in Newport. Dad was an out-of-control alcoholic, and our home life was a nightmare. After he left, our life was so peaceful, in spite of living in government-subsidized housing. Those years made an impression on me that I have never forgotten. I started Rogers High School in 1956, and this is when I met "the girls." I had known several of them in junior high school. We seemed to gel with other girls who had gone to two other junior high schools on Acquidneck Island. Some of us were in classes together, others were in activities together, some of our parents knew each other, and some had been in Catholic schools together since first grade. It was a great mix of young women. We all shared the same values and morals, and one thing was certain—we all loved having a good time. There were scholars, cheerleaders, writers, editors, and athletes, but most of all there were "women in the wings."

We all graduated from high school together in 1959 after years of giggling at pajama parties in various basements and even on a wonderful boat. The summer on the boat was memorable. We all went skinny dipping, but what we didn't know was that our male peers were just waiting in a parking lot for the perfect moment to turn on their headlights. We experimented with smoking and drinking cheap red wine and shared our souls with one another. We walked all over Newport together; there was never an issue of safety. One summer one of the girls worked in a drug store; I can still hear the shrieks of laughter as we drove and parked at Second Beach to experiment with blowing up rubbers, a.k.a. condoms, and let them fly away. We were amazed at the size of them. Anybody who has grown up in Newport will tell you that summer in Newport is the very best; we had so many memorable ones.

After graduation, most went off to college or business school. Because of my mother's financial constraints, I went directly to work for a law firm in town; two years later I went to work for Raytheon. At that time, the girls started to get engaged and get married, several to high school sweethearts, others to Navy men, and others to college sweethearts.

I was one of the last to marry at the old age of twenty-three. I married a Naval officer and left Newport in 1966 for San Diego, Japan, and Hawaii before my husband's retirement to San Diego in 1974. While in San Diego, we had our first child, a fabulous son with his dad's blue eyes and blond hair.

The longest dry spell away from Newport was when we were stationed overseas for three years in Japan. It was an incredibly exciting time in my life, and looking back, the best of the best. We settled into a typical Japanese house, with tatami-mat floors and shoji-screen sliding windows. We had no central heat; during the winter months, we heated one room at a time. I began friendships with my Japanese neighbors three mornings a week, when the vegetable man walked his truck up our hill and we gathered to enjoy the fruits of his labors. I became pregnant right away again and brought home the most wonderful prize of all, a healthy baby boy. Soon after he was born, we moved to base housing. Life was easy, with a live-in maid and a "sew girl" who made all of my clothes using newspapers as patterns. We did a lot of entertaining, and we both also taught conversational English to Japanese students at a private school.

My husband and I did a lot of traveling in and out of the country, and it was a very enriching experience for me. I made Navy friends that I'm still in contact with; we have a real bond.

Coming home was always a priority for me; I never lost touch with my family who were scattered throughout New England. My mother and brother and his family were settled in Newport. My father had passed away shortly after I married. Most of my friends were in Newport as well, and it was always a priority for me to get home and visit with the girls, and oftentimes, their parents. Every visit consisted of meeting new husbands and seeing new babies and kissing my family members. My first trip was from Honolulu with a three- and four-and-a-half-year-old; the three of us flew unaccompanied all the way to Boston with a stopover in San Francisco to change planes. The flight across country found me sitting across the aisle from a priest; in those days, priests were given complimentary cocktails. As he ordered, he said to the hostess, "Give that woman a drink. Lord only knows, she needs one, traveling with those two rascals!"

When we relocated to San Diego in 1974, the four of us came home every other year to visit the grandmothers, family members, and always, "the girls." I have so many happy memories of dinners out and such chatter about our young children and our lifestyles. Those were happy and carefree years—special times at Third Beach with Mrs. Peabody cooking hamburgers and watching our treasured children romp in the ocean.

The year 1984 was a devastating year for me. My husband became ill and died within months, of cancer. I was in shock, in anger, in hate, but eventually was able to pull my priorities together and raise our two sons, who were fifteen and sixteen at the time of their dad's passing. When I think back to those years, it amazes me that I just survived. I was devastated beyond anybody's imagination. I think I always knew that I'd be single forever; one doesn't survive an experience like mine without a broken heart and without the knowledge that the work ahead included being a mom, first and foremost. My boys graduated from high school with honors, went on to college, and eventually married. They have given me five magnificent grandchildren. They are both gainfully employed, one in education and one in business, and they are my proudest product in every possible way. My determination was to get the job done in the best way possible, and I succeeded. They were always first and foremost.

During this journey, I was employed as a part-time receptionist for a small start-up company. Eventually, through the trust of the CEO of this company, I became the human resources director of a 350-person company. I took classes at night, became certified in HR, and loved my job. I traveled, trained, put together benefits packages, and ran the entire department with great pride and one assistant. After I left the company, I ran a small consulting business out of my home for those who were starting up their own small companies. It was a very rewarding experience. I worked directly with the CEOs, training them to solve people problems without meeting any of the employees. I loved it.

In early 2002, I consummated a business deal that resulted in my being able to purchase a small condo on Acquidneck Island, perfectly located between two magnificent beaches and across the street from a private school with beautiful acreage. I'd been dreaming of a way to get back to my roots for years, and my dream had come true. Every year I come home for a month to my little chunk of heaven and am forever grateful for the annual adventure, which always includes seeing the Newport Girls.

Coming home in the 2000 years has consisted of celebrating our children's marriages, becoming grandparents, enjoying retirement, and still loving one another. Recently we celebrated our own private fiftieth high school reunion with several dinners, shopping events, and special times with one another. My most memorable experiences were attending an AA meeting with a loved one and the next day, attending two movies with another loved one. It was special and wonderful.

In closing, my dream is that we will continue to come home together as a group of women who have all had our issues, difficult times, and sadness, but in the end, it's all about friendship, love, acceptance, and mutual respect.

Some of us have giggled about making an early reservation at "the home" before the "big home," all on one floor having wheel chair races. Well, I personally don't know about that, but what I do know is that for as long as I can walk and talk, I'll be coming home.

We're not done yet, girls!

Mary O'Hanley Clark—My Story

It all began many years ago—the Newport Girls, some of us meeting in kindergarten and some in elementary, junior high, and high school. Over the years, we have had several get-togethers—some small, some larger. This year, 2009, was special, for it was fifty years after high school graduation, and so many of us were able to attend—coming from all over the country back to Newport, Rhode Island.

Elaine arrived at my home at approximately 10:30 AM, June 23. The very first thing we had to do was go to the Newport Creamery for a hamburger with red relish. Elaine, along with many others, worked at the Creamery during high school. The Creamery was, and still is, known for its "Awful Awful"—awful big and awful good. If you can drink three, you get one free.

Over the next few days, we had a wonderful time, sharing our innermost feelings and spending much time with the "Newport Girls." Elaine had no idea what an integral part of our group she was and still is. Elaine was out of the box compared to the rest of us. As you read the history, you will see how amazing she is. Because of this week, Elaine has taken on the task of putting together a book for us.

I was born in Newport on October 16, 1941, to Roderick O'Hanley (also born in Newport) and Agatha O'Neil, who was born in Boston. She met my father while vacationing in Newport with a girlfriend. My mother always said, "There is no place like Newport." In 1946, we moved to Middletown, Rhode Island. I have an older and a younger brother. In 1964, I married William E. Clark, a Navy officer from Saginaw, Michigan, who later went to work for Mobil Oil Corporation.

Bill stayed in the Navy reserves for twenty-three years. We were blessed with two daughters—Courtney and Katie. Sadly, Courtney passed away in 1989. Katie is now married and raising her family—three boys and a girl.

As Elaine stated, back fifty years ago, if you were from Newport, Middletown, or Portsmouth, you just said Newport.

All three towns are on Aquidneck Island, which can be reached by one of three bridges depending on where you are coming from. I love telling people that I was baptized at St. Augustine's in the fifth ward of Newport (where many Irish lived and still do); made my first communion at St. Joseph's (Middletown did not have a Catholic church in 1948 so St. Joe's was our parish); was confirmed at St. Lucy's (the new parish in Middletown); and married at Chapel By the Sea—a charming multidenominational church on the Newport Naval Base overlooking beautiful Narragansett Bay.

Now I am a member of St. Mary's in Newport and we live in Portsmouth. I have covered the whole Island and love every aspect of it—from the city to the country and especially the ocean—how I love living by the sea. There were many years we lived off the Island while my husband was working for Mobil Oil. He was transferred many times, mostly in New England.

What can I say? To me, growing up in Newport was wonderful. I was fortunate to have a strong home life with sound guidance. My father owned a Mobil service station and my mother ran the Jack and Jill Nursery School from our home. She later taught at a private kindergarten and then became a social secretary for some of the wealthy who summered in Newport. Eventually she managed the staff of one of the estates.

The "Newport Girls" are all strong and intelligent and very diverse, which makes our getting together through the years so interesting. Many people think if you come from Newport, you must be wealthy. Well, we were not the ones who just summered in Newport. We were the locals, "native Newporters." We wore penny loafers, red, white, and blue Keds and poodle skirts. We did not even know the word "designer." How much each family had was not important to us. We were just friends. We all met through one another. Since we went to different kindergartens, elementary, and junior high schools, the circle continued to grow—all enjoying each other as we added to the group.

Elaine, Arlene, and I spent many Saturdays during junior high at the Portsmouth roller rink. Our parents took turns chauffeuring us "way out to Portsmouth!" We would also frequently ice skate on local ponds.

Eileen had horses and ten brothers and sisters. How I loved going to her house to ride and have dinner at their large dining room table with the whole family. Eileen drove Nancy and me to school every day of our senior year. What fun we had discussing the day's events, and of course, our dates. I remember one day, we drove into the school parking lot and decided we didn't feel like going to school that day. So we turned around and drove to Fall River, Massachusetts (off the Island) and did Christmas shopping. We thought we were "hot stuff." Of course, we spent all day wondering if we would get caught. When I arrived home, I told my mother in case we did get caught, but we didn't. I don't think the school even considered we would do such a thing! Also in our senior year, Eileen and I won the girls' ping-pong tournament.

Many years later while on a cruise, I decided to enter a shipboard ping-pong tourney and was put to shame in minutes. I guess I was not quite the ping-pong pro I thought I was. Nancy and I were cheerleaders, so we spent Saturdays at football games, and Tuesday and Friday evenings at basketball games, with all the other girls cheering our team on.

Now to Ginny. We met in kindergarten. Although we went to different elementary parochial schools, we ended up in junior high and high school together. We met Eileen in junior high and Nancy through Junior Catholic Daughters. Ginny and I spent many nights sleeping over at each other's homes and doing crazy things, hoping to make ourselves look like models. The closest we came was when we were chosen to be Breck Girls. Breck shampoo sponsored a production at the high school featuring hairdos and dress styles through the ages. This did result in a photo story in "Life Magazine," showing us all washing our hair. Unfortunately, we did not get modeling pay.

Summers were spent working and playing. Newport has many beautiful beaches. Every one of us had our favorite beach, so we would spend time at all of them. There was First Beach in Newport, Second and Third Beaches in Middletown, and Gooseberry and Hazard's, also in Newport. The beaches remain and we still enjoy them every chance we get. My summer job was at the well-known Bailey's Beach, where President Kennedy went while summering in Newport.

First and Second had surf. We spent many days waterskiing at Third. Gooseberry and Hazard's had many rocks jutting out ,which we climbed, sunned on, and swam off, resulting in many cut feet. Today, some of the rocks are off limits. I was in the womb at Hazard's and still enjoy being there sixty-eight years later. We all have our favorite spots on the sand, and the alley boys better put our chairs and umbrellas in the right place or they may have to move everything five or ten feet in one direction or the other. When I was growing up, the manager even had an apartment at the beach. He was a wonderful swimmer and gave lessons to all.

Some days, the air and water temperature would be extremely cold, but we had swim lessons no matter what. Hazard's had a great "rock raft" with a diving board. On low-tide days, the diving board was quite high, and of course much closer to the water during high tide, providing an opportunity for a variety of diving tricks. There was a rope with buoy floats that ran from shore out to the rock raft. The rope is still there, but the raft is no longer in use because of years of erosion. In order to go out to the raft without an adult, we had to be able to swim out to the raft and back without holding on to the rope. The adults would think of many things to keep us busy. One activity was to become members of the Super Dolphins Club. Eileen and I, along with many others, qualified as members. To qualify for the Club, you had to be able to swim from Bailey's Beach, out and around the rocks jutting out from Gooseberry Beach, to the shore of Hazard's Beach. During the qualifying swim, you were accompanied by a rowboat. At the west end of the beach is an area with large rocks that jut out of the ocean at low tide. This has always been known as "Crab Town." At low tide, we would play in the water around the rocks and discover all varieties of sea life. Now my grandkids enjoy the fun of "going to Crab Town." To this day, I love the ocean.

The fall was football games and winter was basketball. Our biggest rival was the parochial high school. There were victory balls, proms, parties, parties, and more parties—many we even crashed. Some days and nights, we drove around town with ten to fifteen kids piled in a car, all chipping in for gas. We also did a lot of ice skating in the winter. Kathy's father would light up a local pond on weekends so we could skate at night.

Gretchen would write up all our activities, along with other incidental information, for a weekly column called "Teen Scene" in the *Newport Daily News*. Of course, since Gretchen was one of the "Newport Girls," we were featured regularly. Some others were never mentioned, and they haven't forgotten it fifty years later.

There are so many fond memories of not only the girls but also their families. Ginny's mother made the best English muffin pizzas. Lynn's parents put up with many loud parties. Eileen's served us breakfast after the senior prom. Nancy, Eileen, and Marianne are fortunate to still have their mothers, and we continue to enjoy visiting with them. My own mother did much chauffeuring and listening during those school years. Many afternoons she sat with me and watched the American Bandstand TV show with Dick Clark. She was always awake when I came in at night, waiting to hear what went on. My father and I would have many late-night discussions. While we often did not agree, we enjoyed the talks.

Although we all went our separate ways, we never separated. I believe the relationships have become stronger because we feel fortunate to have each other. When difficulties occurred, we were there for each other. I don't know what I would have done without my friends after our daughter died. My husband and I have always felt that faith, family, and friends are needed to survive tragedies. Nancy, especially, spent hours listening to me, not only after Courtney died but also through the trials and tribulations of marriage, my parent's illnesses and their deaths occurring so close together. Our husbands wondered how we could talk so much—it was easy.

Although the strength of the ties varies from person to person, the "Newport Girls" seem to be connected as one. Perhaps the fact that most of us did leave Newport and became so diverse is what kept us together. I am fully aware that not all Newporters, or other high school girls, had the same experiences we had, which is why the "Newport Girls" are truly blessed. People cannot believe how many of us still talk with, care for, and are around for each other.

As we age, I think we understand even more how lucky we are that the connection hasn't been broken and how much we can laugh at life—the good and the not so good. Oh, sure, we complain at times, but who doesn't? Through the years, we have continued to stay in touch with other classmates from the past and thus have met new friends through each other.

As time takes its toll, which it will, I'm sure we will still be there for each other and will always carry with us our wonderful memories. There is so much more I could say, but most of all, I would just like to say thanks for your friendship and being there when I needed you.

Mary Agatha O'Hanley Clark—one of the lucky "Newport Girls."

Nancy Ellis Carroll—My Story

Friends and family were always the center of my life. I have always loved spending time with my good friends and family. My cousins, childhood friends, neighborhood friends, school friends, and close friends fill a big part of my memory. In my early years, Barbara Nelson and I spent a great deal of time together and had a very special friendship. During my middle school years, I met Mary O'Hanley and Ginny McGinn at Junior Catholic Daughters. Most of my friends were from Newport, and their friends were from Middletown.

When we started our freshman year at Rogers High School, many of our Newport and Middletown friends were combined. For the next four years, we laughed and had fun together. Mary and I still laugh and have fun together. We have remained best friends for more than fifty years.

My best high school experience was meeting Brian. Although I had dated, I was never looking for a serious relationship. A steady boyfriend was the last thing I needed. My father was very controlling and I did not want another person running my life. In the spring of my junior year, I went on my first date with Brian. He was warm and respectful, and quietly confident. In our senior year, we attended most of the dances and social functions together. We both valued our time together and never made any demands. My father placed a lot of restrictions on me, and Brian always respected his wishes. I was not allowed to be in restaurants that served alcohol and had to be home by a specific time. This never became an issue with Brian. Although we never talked about serious commitments, we always felt connected. We both lived our separate lives and valued our time together. Brian did not like mindless conversation. If I talked, he listened and appeared genuinely interested. There were not a lot of phone conversations, but we did talk to one another.

When we headed to college, we had a mutual understanding that we were free to date others. Neither of us had the desire to date others. While attending the University of Rhode Island, Brian would invite me to fraternity weekends. I would stay with Mary at her sorority, which was a real treat for me.

Most weekends, I worked long hours at a drug store. For four years, I worked four days a week and attended Salve Regina College full time. I was taught to be self-sufficient and enjoyed the independence that paying my own way gave me. Any free time was normally spent with Brian.

We were very supportive of one another, and neither of us needed a lot of recognition. After graduation from college, we were married just after Christmas. In March, Brian was commissioned in the U.S. Army. His first assignment was Fort Benning, Georgia. Next was Fort Lewis, Washington, and we drove across country in our little Corvair. For the next two years, Brian was company commander of two hundred young soldiers. After training in Washington, Oregon, and Alaska, Brian was heading to Vietnam. My most vivid memory of Fort Lewis was when the Fourth Infantry Division marched in review just prior to embarking for Vietnam. In that march, Brian led the two hundred young soldiers he would command in Vietnam. I knew that those young men were being led by someone who was quiet, clear thinking, smart, responsible, and clever. Brian was only twenty-five years old.

When Brian returned from Vietnam, he submitted his resignation. He was retained in the service and sent to teach at the University of West Virginia. He was assigned to the ROTC department at the Keyser campus, where he taught military history and tactics. As part of this assignment, Brian was a notification officer for that part of West Virginia. This was an emotionally wrenching assignment. Upon notification from the Pentagon, he would travel to different parts of West Virginia and notify families that their loved one had been killed in Vietnam. He would spend time with the family and make arrangements for a military burial. After the funeral, he would make sure that the families received benefits, etc. The only other problem with this assignment was the paper mill. The small town had a strange odor that came from the mill. Since this is where everyone worked, the locals called it "the sweet smell of money." Other than the notifications and the smell, this was a good time in our young marriage.

While Brian waited to be released from the Army, our second child was born. When our son was only weeks old, Brian received orders to return to Vietnam. This time, he would not be with an American unit. He was heading to the Mekong Delta as an advisor to a Vietnamese unit. I headed back to Rhode Island and rented a small apartment.

After eight months, Brian was finally released from the Army and returned home to start graduate school at URI. A teaching job in the English Department of Portsmouth High followed. I started teaching in the fall at the Maher Center. After taking a year off with our third child, I started teaching in the Newport School Department. Brian and I remained teaching until we retired in 1998.

Our six years in the military gave us a great appreciation of our time together. We learned to appreciate our differences. We are both independent thinkers. I have never felt pressured to change my ways, and I'm sure that Brian feels the same way. We have always found time to laugh and enjoy each other's company. I can't imagine my life without him and I know that we have been great partners. We never stop reminding ourselves how lucky we are. During our fifty years together, the love we discovered in high school has grown and sustained us during difficult times.

Virginia McGinn Regan—My Story

It's June 2009 and the girls have come together for a fiftieth reunion dinner at the Canfield House in Newport, Rhode Island. They have traveled from California, Iowa, North Carolina, Maryland, Florida, Massachusetts, and New Hampshire to join several girls living in Newport. We were celebrating a friendship of more than fifty years, one that could be characterized as unique, or even extraordinary. We were drawn together by our roots in Newport, Rhode Island and our everlasting memories of the good ole days.

We were "the group," the essence of Rogers High School for four years. We were involved in every activity that the school offered, and then some! What one person didn't run or participate in, another did. All aspects of school life were connected through our friendships and involvement with each other and fellow students. We left nothing untouched. We engaged in every activity, for our enjoyment as well as respect for our teachers, fellow students, and Rogers High School.

Where do I begin? School activities included Student Council, Pep Night, cheerleading, yearbook editor and staff, victory ball, senior prom committee and many others. Social activities included parties at Miskiania, Lynn's parties, basketball and football games, and of course, "Teen Scene," a weekly publication written by Gretchen, which was the center of all our activities.

Pep Nite

Pep Nite was an annual variety show, which consisted of two hours of various acts by all interested students. We participated in the formal waltz, the couples' dance routine, and many other acts. The trio of Arlene, Elaine, and Judy brought down the house. The highlight of the evening was the pantomime to the song "Little Darling," by The Three Haircuts.

Breck Girls

Breck Shampoo, in connection with *Colliers Magazine*, came to Rogers High School to produce a fashion show consisting of a variety of clothes ranging from the nineteenth and twentieth centuries. Arlene, Mary, and I were selected to model clothes, along with many other girls.

We rehearsed for several weeks, walking the runway. We were also photographed shampooing our hair in a group picture, which was featured in *Colliers Magazine* as an advertisement for Breck Shampoo. The culmination was a magazine that Breck Shampoo produced, which included all the models. We had a wonderful time and it was a great experience.

Student Council

Students were elected to serve on the Student Council by their peers. Duties included representing the student body to the administration, and organizing activities and social events. Nancy represented the student council as president, and I was vice president.

Miskiania

Miskiania, a beautiful turn-of-the-century Victorian on a private lake, was the spot of our annual two-day escape. Lynn's parents, who acted as chaperones, owned this secluded estate. The girls spent the first day enjoying themselves and their dates joined them the second day. It was a highly anticipated part of our summers.

Lynn's Parties

Lynn's house was the center of many of our activities. We spent many a night there enjoying slumber parties, and also gathered there after basketball and football games with our dates.

Victory Ball

Thanksgiving Day was another day filled with traditions. The day started with everyone attending the Rogers High versus De La Salle football game. Cheering us to victory were Nancy and Mary, cheerleaders for Rogers. After the game dinner with our own families, we would attend the annual Victory Ball, for students of both schools.

Teen Scene

Teen Scene was a weekly publication in the local newspaper that chronicled all of our high school activities. This was written by Gretchen and always included all of our activities and social events, along with those of other student groups. This weekly column kept our names in the limelight.

Even fifty years later, these are the memories that we share that will always remain in our hearts. What drew us together then, still binds us to this day.

Barbara Nelson Watterson—My Story

I first met some of the other Newport Girls in elementary school. Nancy and I go way back—to first grade, I think. Lynn, too. I remember that we—along with Helen Tobak and Georgette Ramos and a few others—formed a group when we were about nine or ten years old. At Georgette's suggestion, it was called the Friday Afternoon Fish and Beer Club. I must have been the secretary, because I still have some meeting minutes. We met on Tuesdays—go figure.

Our "gang" expanded its membership when the Middletowners joined us in ninth grade, and I got to know the rest of the Newport Girls. I remember being really proud to be in the same crowd as the very popular Haircuts when they became an instant sensation at Pep Nite. Because I was an only child, it was always important to me to have friends, and I appreciated being a part of the "in crowd" at Rogers High School. In what was an outstanding class, our little group stood out: cheerleaders, student council members, editors of *The Red and Black*, *Teen Scene*, and the yearbook—the list is long. We were special.

One thing that I especially liked about our gang—and that I didn't realize until long after high school graduation—was how diverse it was in a sociological sense. We came from a wide range of households, and yet I doubt if any of us really thought about that at the time. We were just happy to have fun with one another, regardless of where we lived, what religion we practiced, or what kind of job(s) our parents had.

I returned to Newport after college and taught when my three daughters—Julie, Kate, and Beth—were young, and then we moved from Newport in 1980. Although my husband Jim's architectural projects have necessitated our having a second home in many interesting places, we have owned our old house in Westport for nearly twenty years.

That location has been an anchor for us, and it has brought me back into closer contact with the Newport Girls, thanks in large part to Nancy and Mary, who always let me know when there will be a fun get-together.

It's my observation that our relatively small group of women represents a microcosm of society. Among us, we have experienced many of life's major personal events—both happy and tragic—and we have been there for one another during those times.

We have also lived through huge world changes. Who, in 1959, would have dreamed that we would be able to send instant messages or speak by phone from virtually anywhere, that there would be no Soviet Union and one unified Germany, that there would be two female Supreme Court justices, a female Secretary of State, and a black president of the United States? It's hard to fathom.

I savor this time in my life. I am grateful for the good health that enables me to enjoy my passions—my family, which now includes five beautiful grandchildren, travel, tennis, and my great love of classical choral music.

And I am especially happy to share —for fifty plus years and counting— strong and enduring friendships with my fellow grandmothers, who are still and who will always be—the Newport Girls.

Lynn Harvey Summers—My Story

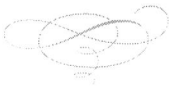

I grew up in Newport, Rhode Island. There were five of us in our family—my mother, my father, my sister Anne, and my brother Bill. We lived in a rented apartment until I was in third grade, when my parents built a two-story colonial home. Little did I know at the time that this would be such a wonderful gathering place for me and my friends during our teenage years (pajama parties, boy-girl parties, and just hanging out).

It was in 1956 when I went to Rogers High School that the "Newport Girls" met and became friends for life. It escapes me how we all came together as friends—we were from all different parts of the island. There were about twelve to fifteen of us who regularly got together, and most of us have stayed in touch all these years.

At the beginning of this summer, we had our own mini fiftieth high school reunion. Twelve of us met for dinner. I hadn't seen Elaine in about eighteen years (the others I had seen on a fairly regular basis). We just picked up where we left off—had lots of hugs, laughs, and non-stop conversations.

Some of the fondest memories of our high school years occurred at Miskiania Camp (a magical place my parents had access to). We would usually go there one weekend per year. The girls would spend the first night, and the boys would come over the next day for a cookout. My mother and Mrs. Gately (Sally's mom) were our chaperones. They were wonderful to put up with such a bunch of giddy girls. One time, we went through the woods to a field of blueberry bushes and picked enough blueberries to make pies for dessert.

Elaine Colton

After graduation in 1959, we all went our separate ways—some stayed in Newport, others went off to college—but we stayed in touch and got together mostly in the summer. I think we all felt safe, comfortable, and happy to have such a special friendship throughout our lives.

I'm sure there are more good times to come.

Eileen O'Reilly Daschbach—My Story

It was with great anxiety that I entered the old Rogers High School as a midyear sophomore transfer student. As a young fourteen–year-old coming from a small, all-girls' school to a maze of stairwells, hallways, and half-story annexes, it took me a while to fit in. It was very embarrassing to arrive at classes late, especially since there were boys in this school. It has occurred to me that many a Navy student has had to face similar difficulties, perhaps even twice during their moves during high school. Fortunately for me, there were some friends from grammar school who welcomed me.

They had already joined together with a number of other girls to form quite a large, bubbly group. We all know how important "the group" is at that age, and I was very lucky to be included so quickly. It made such a difference to be able to walk down the halls with old and new friends, and before long, the difficult time of transition was over. It was quite a new beginning for all of us to move to the new, fancy school, and we have many a picture in the yearbook showing us crowded together in hallways and lunchrooms. Of course, there were all the parties and summers together also.

My dear friend Mary is the one I knew the longest and spent the most time with during grammar and high school. I have her to thank for always keeping me informed about everyone over the years. I was very happy that we were all able to come together for dinner after more than fifty years. That we all wanted to see each other and continue laughing and catching up says a lot about our enduring friendships. It seems that such a large group has stayed close because of acceptance without conditions and judgments. It is a mystery to me why we have all lived

Elaine Colton

this long and I am very thankful we have had this time to appreciate and value one another and look forward to many more gatherings.

Linda Simmons—My Story

What do I remember?

I remember riding around with more friends than seats, and helping out with gas in change. I remember us stopping and getting a "hot chez." I remember sitting in the back seat of the Harveys' car with our crinolines up to our chins as Mr. Harvey drove us to school. I remember meeting in the halls before class as Gretchen shouted out her greeting. I remember that we had to have shampoo in our hair for the pictures of us as Breck Girls for *Life* magazine. It was my first time seeing a boys' bathroom. I remember our hiking trip to hanging rock.

I remember being fascinated that Mary could bend the way she did, to do a cheer. I remember us using Lynn's sunlamp to get a tan before the prom, and some of us, including me, getting way too much. I remember that some of us wondered if Billy McCann and I kissed, would we make "sparks," because we both wore braces. I remember a slumber party on Lynn's sailboat and trying hard to lift "the skinny dippers" back into the boat before the boys swam out. I remember Miskiania and the fun we had there. I remember the ferry and Margot—the blonde with the bongos who invited us to a party on the ferry. I remember Pep Nite and "You Are So Rare to Me." Elaine, Arlene, and Judy were great! I remember how neat I thought it was that we had two years at the old Rogers and two years at the new.

I remember the Newport Creamery, and the "awful awfuls," and the medium-rare hamburgers that were so juicy they'd squirt you in the eye when you bit down on them. I remember the drive-in and Tommy's Diner. I remember all the parties in Lynn's basement. I want to give kudos to Lynn and her family— if it wasn't for their caring love and hospitality, we would have missed out on a lot of good memories.

Thoughts of Today

It is quite remarkable that after these many years, everyone in the "crowd" (and we were a crowd) has never been forgotten, even though some of us have not had any contact with each other on a regular basis. We all go back to that magical time of the fifties at Rogers High. By the way, does anyone know the exact head count? I never even thought of us as "a crowd" until someone asked if she could join. Well, I looked at her like a dog with a new pan. I never looked at us like that—we were just us—each with our own individuality and different backgrounds, coming together to have good, clean fun!

There's another thing I never thought of until I got older, and that was that I was from a dysfunctional family. Who would have thought? But we never discussed what went on in our homes; and life was life and you were there and that was it. But I was always "there" when I was in the crowd, and it was wonderful to be accepted for who I was. When I stepped into "there," well, it was a safe place, an accepted place, and a fun place to be.

I didn't realize how unusual it was and how blessed we were to have friendships like we had, that would last forever.

Kathy Ewart Keay—My Story

Some Background

I was born in February 1942 to Jennie Occaso and William Cronin Ewart, the only daughter among four children. Mom was a telephone operator for New England Telephone and Telegraph and spent many years as a Federation representative—which is similar to a union shop steward—before Ma Bell was officially unionized. Dad was a master electrician and foreman for Harry Groff Contractors. Both were born in Newport. Mom was first-generation Italian-American, and dad was second-generation Irish and Scots.

I mention ethnic background because it was important in Newport in those days, more so than other towns I've lived in. Newport society had something of a class system in which certain ethnic/religious groups were deemed to be of higher status than others, but with our group, class and status made no difference.

Mom and Dad built the first house on our street (Florence Avenue), bringing electricity, water, and other utilities into our neighborhood. In fact, most of the land in the neighborhood belonged to various estates before being broken into parcels for sale. Growing up, we had an estate next door and another one at the end of Florence Avenue. Behind us was undeveloped land owned by another estate. Of course, now it has all been developed, but as kids we sure had fun building forts and hiding out on estate property. I was a few months old when we moved into 19 Florence Avenue. Our neighborhood is in the "fighting fifth" ward, so named because of the many Irish who settled there and who were known to drink a wee bit too much and to get into a few too many brawls.

When mom died a few years back, my brother Tom bought the house from the rest of us—me, Bill, and Dick. Two "Newport Girls" were of invaluable help—Marianne and Mary. Marianne provided us with a model real estate contract, and Mary gave us the names of attorneys.

Even after many years of my not being in touch with either one, they both eagerly volunteered assistance. That is why the "Newport Girls" are so unique. We've always been there for each other—no matter what.

Our Beginning

The "Newport Girls" came together as a unit while we were attending Rogers High School, although some of us met in elementary school, and some before. But it was in high school that we really got to know each other and formed a bond of friendship that has endured to this day.

Looking back, the very first "Newport Girl" I got to know was Marianne Del Nero (Johnson), who lived just down the street from our house. We spent much of our childhood playing together at each other's homes. Marianne's mom made the best cookies. I remember Christmas mornings after church, we would run to each other's house to show each other what Santa had brought us. When we entered St. Augustine's Parochial Elementary School, we cemented a friendship with another "Newport Girl," Mary McAloon (Watanabe)." Mary lived across the street from Rogers High School in a barn (actually, a converted livery stable) that had been part of one of the estates. Mary was always ready when one of the teachers yelled at her, "Close the door, do you live in a barn?" to respond with "Yes, I do!" Sleepovers at Mary's were always a treat—listening to the fog horns as they lulled us to sleep. Once during high school, Mary held a pajama party for all the girls in one of the large vacant rooms in the barn—it was a blast!

High School Years

Attending Rogers High School was a real awakening—quite a different atmosphere from that of St. Augustine's—and did I love it! I thrived and blossomed there. Thinking about our times at Rogers brings back so many pleasant memories. I also recall some embarrassing memories—but that's another book!

The first of the "Newport Girls" to get her driver's license—and thus access to the family car—was Lynn Harvey (Summers).

On her first attempt to drive the gang over to visit another "Newport Girl," Sally Gately (Richardson), Lynn didn't quite make it thru the stone gates at the entrance to the drive and had a lot of explaining to do. High school years were so enriched by knowing Lynn and her family. I recall one summer, in exchange for helping clean her family's boat, we all got a nice, long sail after we were finished—a bargain at any price! Then there was the time we had a pajama party on the boat anchored at Ida Lewis Yacht Club and went skinny dipping under a moonless sky. We didn't notice the group of our male friends swimming silently up to the boat until Lynn's parents shone their car's large spotlight on them. What a scramble to get up the ladder and get covered!

We'd cruise up and down Broadway looking for other high school friends to meet up with and always rendezvoused at Tommy's Diner—everyone's favorite hangout. I had a 1940 Oldsmobile coupe—the kind with the running boards, the starter button above the gas pedal, and a choke—with a back seat large enough that friends could pile in three layers deep. One day leaving school, fourteen of us piled into the car, but we got only as far as the street outside Rogers High School. A traffic policeman stopped us and asked us to unpack ourselves. What a reliable old car she was.

Lucky for, us many of our parents, mine included, let us hold parties. In the summer, my dad would string paper Japanese lanterns in our back yard and make pizzas. "Newport Girl" Gretchen Buxbaum (Kelly) always said she loved my father's pizzas best. During the winter when the pond near Rogers High School was frozen over, my dad would borrow a huge spotlight and a generator from the electric company and light up the pond; Mom always supplied the hot chocolate. That's how we did things in Newport—no permission slips from city hall, just good will.

Newport was a party town—not in the sense it means today, but parties hosted by parents for their children and their children's friends. Lynn always had us over and we'd find our way to her basement, where we rocked and rolled to the best of the fifties sounds. One year after a football game between Rogers and De La Salle—our rival in town—I invited a number of friends to my house for a party.

The word quickly spread, as it always did, and we had kids from both schools packed wall-to-wall on our first floor. With instructions from Mom to winnow out the party crashers, I escorted them out the front door—and Dad was letting them back in through the back door. It was rather funny now that I recall it.

Then there was the time that almost the entire school skipped classes and went bowling at Aquidneck Lanes. It happened on a horrible, icy, snowy day—a day that school should have been canceled but wasn't. In fact, so few teachers and students actually made it to school, there were no classes—just large study groups. Our school superintendent, when determining whether or not to call a snow day and close the schools, made the decision based on how difficult it would be for a little girl to have to walk to school in the snow and ice.

Our principal, however, took exception with the superintendent's peculiar decision-making rubric, and during morning announcements snidely remarked, "I wonder where that little girl is now." That did it! I suggested to just a few friends that we skip school and go to my house for the day.

We had never skipped before, but that day it seemed the right thing to do. However, as things do in small towns, the word quickly spread about a party at my house and the school just about emptied. Eventually, we all ended up at the bowling alley. But the next day, Ms. Carr (the girls' guidance counselor) called me out and was very angry with me, as if I had orchestrated a mutiny or something. Why she thought I was responsible, I'll never know.

Summer time was always beach time. Those of us who were members of Gooseberry Beach would scramble over the rocks to Hazard's beach and meet up with Mary O'Hanley (Clark), "Riles"—Eileen O'Reilly (Daschbach), Sally Gately (Richardson), and others. But we also haunted Second and Third Beaches, where at night we had bonfires and gathered with other members of the crew—Ginny, Judy, Arlene, Elaine, Lynn, Linda, Eileen, and Nancy, to name a few.

Summer also meant the Newport Jazz Festival, where we heard some of the greatest jazz musicians of all time—Louis "Satchmo" Armstrong, who celebrated his July 4 birthday every year, Duke Ellington, Count Basie, Gerry Milligan, Ella Fitzgerald, Miles Davis, Stan Getz, and many others. We were very privileged to have been there during those times.

Unfortunately, the Jazz Festival that George Wein started in '54 changed drastically during the sixties. Both the music and the crowds changed—especially the crowds, who became increasingly rowdy and drugged up. It got so bad that the true jazz musicians no longer wanted to play at the festival. They were replaced by musicians with different interpretations of jazz and different sounds, and eventually the festival moved from Newport to Madison Square Garden in New York. I don't know if the New York venue was able to return the festival to its initial commitment to pure jazz, but when jazz was at its height, we heard it.

Talking about talent, one year during the Rogers annual talent show, Elaine Glickman (Colton), Arlene Callahan (Dovel), and Judy White (Rafferty) had the audience screaming for more with their lip-syncing performance of "You Are so Rare." So they rushed home to get another record and did an encore later the same evening for another huge round of applause.

The "Newport Girls," as Elaine has dubbed us, pretty much ran Rogers High School, when I think about it. We were very involved in so many school activities: club officers, student council officers, cheerleaders, choir and band members. If you look in our yearbook, you'd see long lists of activities under our names. We were fortunate to attend a high school that encouraged our growth in so many ways. And we were fortunate to have each other—we had a support system, although we didn't know then that's what it was called.

Moving On

After high school, some stayed in Newport and others moved away. Linda, Ginny, Nancy, and I attended Salve Regina College in Newport and continued our friendship. Whenever one of the girls returned for a visit or semester break, we all gathered to catch up.

After college, I left for Boston to begin a career in fashion merchandising, and within a year, I married Karl Keay, a career naval officer. As a military family, we lived in Hawaii, Virginia Beach, and Falls Church, VA (a suburb of Washington DC), where I settled for twenty-four years. Our marriage lasted eleven years and produced two wonderful kids—David and Debbie.

It was in DC that I met and married my second husband, Robert Duncan, a career CIA officer. We've been married now for over thirty years and it looks like it is going to stick. I worked in various careers while in DC, but when Robert retired in 1995 we left for the B-E-A-C-H—as in Holden Beach, North Carolina. But after three hurricanes in four years passing through our living room, we said "uncle" and headed for higher ground. We settled in Greensboro, North Carolina, where Robert teaches at Guilford College and I'm having fun with stock trading.

Ellen Parsonage Wright
—Crossing over the Newport Bridge

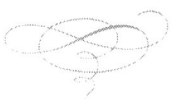

I was born on the Acquidneck Island in Newport, Rhode Island on September 9, 1941. I have been married to Graham Wright for forty-eight years, and we have two children and five grandchildren. I became acquainted with the Newport Girls in high school. It was a very large group of girls who came from different social and economic backgrounds. We were typical teenagers, enjoying good times and weathering the boy-girl problems that arose from time to time. Our gatherings were always centered around the Harveys' house on Catherine Street. We hung out with the girls and tried to solve all of our teenage problems, handing out free advice about boys, etc., and having great sleepovers. There could be two or twenty boys and girls in the recreation room, dancing, making out, and having a great time. I wonder to this day how Mr. and Mrs. Harvey kept their sanity, but somehow they managed.

We would take many trips to Hazard's Beach, ogling the lifeguards, water skiing, and enjoying the sun. Nancy, one of the Newport Girls, married her first love, Brian, who was one of the lifeguards. We branched out and left the Island, which many Islanders never do in a lifetime. Jamestown was our destination, heading to Miskiania, a log cabin on a lake in the woods. Teenagers in the woods with no TV should have caused a ruckus; however, quite the opposite occurred. We entertained ourselves, which was not hard to do, with swimming, canoeing, exploring, and cooking out.

Sometimes it was just girls, and other times it was girlfriends and boyfriends. The setting was quite rustic and the accommodations quite simple—girls on the second-floor dorm and boys on the first-floor dorm, with the chaperones in between. To my knowledge, it worked out well. All these experiences were quite conducive to preparing us for committed, lasting friendships.

After graduation, we all headed in different directions. Mine took me off the island to Arlington, Virginia, where I lived for thirty years with my husband Graham and our children until they went off to college. This did not end my Newport days, because every year we would return to Newport with our family for a week-long vacation. As the girls got older, they would bring girlfriends, and later girlfriends were replaced by boyfriends.

Coming over the Newport Bridge was always awe-inspiring, and you knew you were going home, albeit for a short time. In 1993, my husband retired and we bought a house in Portsmouth, Rhode Island. Naturally my girls continued to visit, bringing husbands and children. At this time, I continued to visit Miskiania with my cousin Betty Lou Oakley, who married my friend Lynn Harvey's brother, Billy.

The adult memories were the same as the earlier memories, creating a time warp. In 2004, my husband and I moved to Florida. The Newport visits briefly ended for the first time in my life but continued on after a three year gap. Crossing the Newport Bridge still brings back the same fond memories I have always had. Most likely, someday a portion of my ashes will be spread around the Ocean Drive.

The End

Someone said I have to "end" this tale. I don't know how to! How do you end the experience of sharing the story of these wonderful girls? We are all still a work in progress. It's not over till it's over!

I do have a deeper appreciation of what it is to take on life, with all the bumps and curves in the road and somehow, stay connected to people who helped shape your life. I still love who everyone was and is. No circumstances can change that.

Epilogue

This tale of my journey, made richer by the great ladies who touched me, was made just a little sweeter by those girls who took my invitation to heart and shared their stories as well. Not everyone wanted to do that. Who cares? One cherishes what one has.

A deep appreciation for the Newport Girls who helped me make this book a reality: Arlene Callahan Dovel, Gretchen Buxbaum Kelly, Mary O'Hanley Clark, Nancy Ellis Carroll, Lynn Harvey Summers, Barbara Nelson Watterson, Eileen O'Reilly Daschbach, Ellen Parsonage Wright, Virginia McGinn Regan, Linda Simmons, and Kathy Ewart Keay. A huge thank you to Sally Gately Richardson, who pointed me in the right direction.

A special thanks to my dear friends Susan Raine, Sharon Toepfer Burns, Marti Burton, and my love forever, Rick Leeds, who are not part of the Newport Girls but gave generously of their time to offer thoughts, edits, and advice.

Elaine Glickman Guber Bergoffen Colton

The original Newport Girl who started it all